Coxey's Army

Witness to History

Peter Charles Hoffer and Williamjames Hull Hoffer, Series Editors

ALSO IN THE SERIES:

Tim Lehman, *Bloodshed at Little Bighorn: Sitting Bull, Custer, and the Destinies of Nations*

Williamjames Hull Hoffer, *The Caning of Charles Sumner: Honor, Idealism, and the Origins of the Civil War*

Daniel R. Mandell, *King Philip's War: Colonial Expansion, Native Resistance, and the End of Indian Sovereignty*

Erik R. Seeman, *The Huron-Wendat Feast of the Dead: Indian-European Encounters in Early North America*

Peter Charles Hoffer, *When Benjamin Franklin Met the Reverend Whitefield: Enlightenment, Revival, and the Power of the Printed Word*

William Thomas Allison, *My Lai: An American Atrocity in the Vietnam War*

Peter Charles Hoffer, *Prelude to Revolution: The Salem Gunpowder Raid of 1775*

Michael Dennis, *Blood on Steel: Chicago Steelworkers and the Strike of 1937*

Donald R. Hickey, *Glorious Victory: Andrew Jackson and the Battle of New Orleans*

John R. Van Atta, *Wolf by the Ears: The Missouri Crisis, 1819–1821*

Coxey's Army

POPULAR PROTEST IN
THE GILDED AGE

BENJAMIN F. ALEXANDER

Johns Hopkins University Press | Baltimore

Johns Hopkins University Press
2715 North Charles Street
Baltimore, Maryland 21218-4363
www.press.jhu.edu

Library of Congress Cataloging-in-Publication Data

Alexander, Benjamin F., 1962–
    Coxey's army : popular protest in the gilded age / Benjamin F. Alexander.
        pages cm. — (Witness to history)
    Includes bibliographical references and index.
    ISBN 978-1-4214-1620-5 (hardcover : alk. paper) — ISBN 1-4214-1620-4
(hardcover : alk. paper) — ISBN 978-1-4214-1621-2 (pbk. : alk. paper)
 — ISBN 1-4214-1621-2 (pbk. : alk. paper) — ISBN 978-1-4214-1622-9
(electronic) — ISBN 1-4214-1622-0 (electronic) 1. Coxey's Army—History.
2. Labor movement—United States—History—19th century. 3. Unemployed
—United States—Political activity—History—19th century. 4. Coxey, Jacob
Sechler, 1854–1951. 5. Working class—United States. I. Title.
    HD8072.A314 2015
    331.880973'09034—dc23
                          2014020801

A catalog record for this book is available from the British Library.

Special discounts are available for bulk purchases of this book. For
more information, please contact Special Sales at 410-516-6936 or
specialsales@press.jhu.edu.

Johns Hopkins University Press uses environmentally friendly book
materials, including recycled text paper that is composed of at least
30 percent post-consumer waste, whenever possible.

To Muriel Broadman, fellow author and dear friend

CONTENTS

Coxey's Army

Prologue
May 1, 1894

"ATTENTION COMMONWEAL. FORWARD, MARCH!"

Riding on his Percheron stallion, wearing buckskin frontier attire with the added formal touch of a necktie, Marshal Carl Browne issued the order at 10:15 a.m., the first of May, 1894. The procession of riders, wagons, and at least 600 unemployed men traveling on foot, known as the Commonweal of Christ, began moving out of Brightwood Riding Park toward the Capitol district of Washington, DC. The Goddess of Peace led the way: 17-year-old Mamie Coxey, mounted atop a white stallion, adorned with an all-white riding habit, blue cap, and stylish parasol. Behind her rode her father, "General" Jacob S. Coxey, in a fancy black carriage with his second wife, Henrietta, and their two-month-old baby boy, Legal Tender Coxey. Another carriage carried Annie L. Diggs, a prominent member of the Populist Party from Kansas, along with a few of her family members. A young cowboy known as "Oklahoma Sam" showed off his talent for riding a pony seated backwards. The general's 18-year-old son, Jesse, also rode in the procession, sporting the colors of blue and grey to symbolize the nation's healing from the Civil War three decades earlier. The "soldiers" of this "industrial army" carried wooden rods with white banners, each one declaring the Commonweal's slogan, "Peace on earth; good will toward men, but death to interest on bonds."[1]

They started out on a dusty road, then paraded down Fourteenth Street. Spectators by the thousands, as well as uniformed police, lined the route. The Commonweal passed the Treasury building, which police and federal troops guarded with extra vigilance, then turned onto Pennsylvania Avenue and headed toward the Capitol. An even heavier concentration of spectators and law enforcers awaited them there. At the B Street entrance to the Capitol grounds, Browne ordered the marchers to halt, dismounted his horse, and escorted the young goddess to repose under the shade of a nearby maple tree. Coxey kissed his wife—this drew cheers in itself—and emerged from the carriage. In his pocket, he carried the script of a speech. Now came the long-awaited moment of truth. As everyone present knew, he intended to ascend the steps of the Capitol and deliver that speech to the crowd. As everybody also knew, the police stood poised to stop him.

The march of Coxey's Army had begun on Easter Sunday, March 25 that year, in Coxey's hometown of Massillon, Ohio. Perhaps as many as a hundred men had made most or all of the march. Newspaper readers nationwide had followed their trek through Ohio, Pennsylvania, and Maryland, learning the names of the colorful characters among them—"Oklahoma Sam," the "Great Unknown," "Weary Bill" Iler—and the rifts and squabbles that had at times threatened to break up the venture. People had read of the reception the Commonwealers met with from townspeople along the way, as well as the preparations that capital city authorities were making for their arrival. The general public also understood that, even as Coxey and Browne and their followers strode down Fourteenth Street that day, hundreds more, maybe even thousands, were on their way from all over the country to join them.

The United States was in the second year of a severe economic depression. Unemployment had reached the dangerously high rate of 20 percent, and many workers who still had their jobs were seeing their wages cut. Stories of desperation abounded. When the Commonweal arrived in Washington, nearly all the nation's coal miners, whose union president, John McBride, was a friend of Coxey's, were on strike, hoping that the resulting coal shortage would raise prices and thus restore some stability to their earnings. A labor dispute over pay cuts at the Pullman Palace Car Company in Illinois was about to bring another ally of the "general," Eugene V. Debs, onto the national stage as the leader of the country's railroad workers in a refusal to

The Coxeyites setting out from Brightwood Riding Park, May 1, 1894. LC-USZ62-96526, Library of Congress, Washington, DC.

work on trains that carried Pullman cars. While this triad of events unfolded and while general misery spread and worsened, newspapers and magazines printed reams of opinions as to why the crisis had hit, and what governments, businesses, and charities should do about it.

Coxey's Army represented one such opinion: that Congress should launch a massive project of building and repairing roads around the nation, specifically employing the unemployed for the task; and that it should finance the venture by issuing $500 million of paper money to state and county governments, $20 million per month, in exchange for non-interest-bearing bonds that those governments would be allowed to issue. Jacob Coxey published a newspaper titled *Good Roads*, and he had lobbied for his proposal in the more traditional way before leading this march. He believed that this simple measure would accomplish several goals dear to his heart: alleviating unemployment, improving the roads, and expanding the currency. Like the striking coal and railroad workers, the marchers in Coxey's Army were members of the work force who felt that, if they were ready and willing to work productively, then by rights they should be able to make a living by doing so; and that, if impersonal market forces did not afford them this opportunity, they were entitled to a remedy from their government. That so many roads throughout the country waited to be either built or repaired made the remedy obvious to the Coxeyites. They were now marching to the Capitol to point this out to Congress.

Coxey's Good Roads plan stood no chance of passing, or even receiving serious debate. While Congress had taken some steps in recent years toward regulating big business, in the form of bringing railroad rates and corporate monopolies under control, it showed no inclination to involve itself directly in providing relief to the poor or setting up public works projects for the purpose of creating jobs. Indeed, such proposals often drew rebuffs even at the local level. To many, the plan Coxey proposed seemed radical. So did the manner of delivery. Rallies and rebellions, both peaceful and not so peaceful, had certainly occurred before, but never had such large bands of protesters from around the country converged on Washington to air their demands. The First Amendment, as everyone knew, guaranteed the right of the people to assemble and petition the government, but did this include the right to converge on the Capitol grounds and deliver speeches from the Capitol steps? According to capital city authorities at the time, it did not.

Though unprecedented in a number of ways, the feeling behind the 1894 march of Coxey's Army did not materialize from nowhere. It grew out of years of economic and social change in which many laboring Americans believed that their lives had passed from their own hands to unresponsive, outside forces. It grew out of the intense suffering that Americans experienced after the collapse of the economy in 1893. The march of Coxey's Army came as the physical manifestation of the long annals of debate over inequities in the American economic order and the proper role of government in response to economic privation. It also came as one in a series of events that made 1894 generally a year of upheaval and unease for Americans.

1 The Gilding of an Age

Jacob Coxey knew both the joys and the sorrows of America's industrial era. His father, Thomas Coxey, worked in a sawmill in Selinsgrove, Pennsylvania, at the time of his birth in 1854. When Jacob was 6, the family moved to Dannville, Pennsylvania, where Thomas took a job at an iron mill. Jacob, educated in the public schools with at least one additional year at a private academy, went to work at the mill as a water boy at 16 (by which time his father had the title of engineer), then worked his way up to machine oiler, boiler tender, and finally engineer. But at age 19, he experienced the impact of the depression of 1873, which closed down the mill for some length of time. As he later recalled, the community had to use artificial scrip for currency, real money being scarce. Still, the Coxey family did not suffer nearly as much as many others did. In 1878 Jacob entered a partnership with an uncle in the scrap-iron business in Harrisburg.[1]

An avid reader, Coxey may have read the book that gave that time period its enduring nickname. Mark Twain and Charles Dudley Warner published their novel *The Gilded Age: A Tale of Today* in 1873. Their story of the Hawkins family from Tennessee did not anticipate the extent of industrial development or the labor and class conflicts that dominated American life over the next several decades; it did, however, colorfully depict the greed of land speculators and the crookedness of urban machine politicians. It suggested, as many of its readers clearly felt, that a once-virtuous society stood in danger of losing its soul to the love of money. The authors' choice of the word *gilded*, referring to the process of using a thin layer of gold to make an ordinary object look ornate and expensive, carried a clear message in itself: that the America of their day fell short of its outer appearances and high ideals.

The Gilded Age was an age of transformations. In the 1890s, though most of its population still farmed, the United States had fully taken its place among the world's leading industrial powers. In 1890, it produced 4.2 million tons of steel, up from 68,700 in 1870, and 22 million barrels of oil, up from 1869's 3.2 million. Railroad tracks fanning out across the country came to more than 166,000 miles in 1890, having stretched only to 79,000 in 1877. Steel, oil, and railroads helped propel one another's growth. Building trains and tracks required steel. Locomotives, though fueled first by wood and later by coal, required oil for lubrication. The oil and steel industries, like most others, needed trains to transport first the raw materials for processing and then the processed goods for distribution. These and other industries propelled the United States from being the fourth largest industrial power in 1860, behind Britain, France, and Germany, to number one in 1900, surpassing the output of those other three combined.[2]

Industrialism also elevated a small number of men, whether by resourcefulness, luck, or guile, to great wealth. Andrew Carnegie, whose Scottish family immigrated when he was 13, acquired his fortune by building up an empire making steel. Pioneering the art of "vertical integration," he saved expenses in the long term by acquiring ownership and control of every part of the process, from mining the iron ore to distributing the finished products. Augustus Swift and Philip Armor did likewise with the processing and packing of meat in the Midwest. John D. Rockefeller entered the oil refining industry and then combined vertical integration with horizontal, forcing competitors to merge with him or go under, which earned him the nickname "Wreck-a-fellow." The railroads produced a number of legendary names: Collis P. Huntington, a leading investor in the first transcontinental railroad and later president of Southern Pacific; Jay Gould, whose empire included not only many railroad lines but also, for a time, Western Union; and Leland Stanford, a Central Pacific Railroad executive who also served as California's governor and then U.S.

senator and who founded the university that still bears his name. Alongside them all, J. P. Morgan grew enormously rich as one of the leading investment bankers, increasingly powerful at century's end, as industrial capitalism evolved into finance capitalism.

With industrialization came the growth of cities. Since the early nineteenth century, New England had textile centers in Lowell and Lawrence, Massachusetts, and Providence, Rhode Island. Lynn, Massachusetts, had become a shoemaking center by 1860. For major port cities like Boston, New York, Philadelphia, and Baltimore, the waterfront itself made those cities thriving import-export centers and also, because commerce generally runs on credit, seats of banking. Garment making and printing also played a big part in the growth of New York and Philadelphia. On the western end of Pennsylvania sat Pittsburgh, whose glass and iron industries, as well as railroad lines and its position along the Ohio River, made it a major city at mid-century. After the Civil War, Pittsburgh and the surrounding region grew further with steel. Western Pennsylvania's mines supplied both iron ore for the steel industry and coal to fuel the trains and heat the homes of much of the country. Eastern Pennsylvania also had its metal works, including the iron mill in Danville, which employed Thomas and Jacob Coxey. Cincinnati and Chicago, situated in the agricultural heartland of the Midwest, came of age in large part through farm machinery and meat-packing plants.[3]

At every step, advances in technology helped speed things up. Interchangeable parts made large-scale manufacturing much more efficient. In the early nineteenth century, to complete the making of a rifle, a clock, or any other kind of complex machinery, a skilled fitter had to sit at his workbench with all the parts in front of him and shave them with a metal file before they could be put together. After Eli Whitney, Samuel Colt, and others developed the technology for interchangeable parts—the ability to churn out parts calibrated to a precise size and shape, ready to assemble without any shaving—workers could now build clocks, rifles, and sewing machines in far greater quantity. The sewing machine, in turn, made possible the mass production of ready-made clothing. New uses of electricity abounded. By the 1890s, much of the country already had electric lights and electric local passenger trains, though long-distance rail carriers still ran on coal.[4]

The nation itself grew considerably during these years. By 1890 whites, including many European immigrants, had settled west of the Mississippi and created states all over the West, including Colorado, the Dakotas, Montana, and Idaho. The territory of Utah, settled as early as 1847 by Mormons, had an unusually long probationary period before becoming a state in 1896, owing largely to conflicts over polygamy. (Mormon church authorities renounced the practice in 1890.) After 1890, only three territories on the continent awaited their statehood: Oklahoma (formerly Indian Territory, just now opening up to white settlement), New Mexico, and Arizona.[5]

Jacob Coxey, though never anywhere near Rockefeller's league, found a niche in America's industrial revolution. In 1881, while he was still in partnership with his uncle in the scrap-iron firm and married to his first wife, Caroline, one of his routine business trips took him to the up-and-coming town of Massillon, Ohio. He liked Massillon so much, he decided to make it his home. He bought a sizable farm, and then built a quarry to produce a grade of silica sand usable in the glass and iron industries. He made a name for himself in another enterprise, too: breeding race horses for one of the country's most popular spectator sports at the time. He also came to enjoy betting on horses, a little too much for Caroline's tastes: she left him in 1888, after fourteen years of marriage. They had four children, at least two of whom played roles in Coxey's Army.[6]

Faces of Inequality

Not everybody in the United States could celebrate the nation's post–Civil War growth. White expansion and the creation of those new western states meant repudiation of treaties previously made with Native Americans, leading to bloody wars and massacres. Regions where the indigenous population had continued to follow their way of life before the Civil War, including the formally designated "Indian Territory," became the new frontier for white expansion, especially when settlers discovered gold. In numerous instances across the Plains, skirmishes between natives and settlers escalated to full-scale war. Ultimately, in key settlement areas, the U.S. Army's objective became that of compelling natives to relocate to reservations. When whites and Indians faced each other on the battlefields, the Indians had the short-term advantages and could inflict much damage, but in the long run the technology, discipline, and manpower of the army prevailed. Meanwhile, the depletion of the buffalo herd wiped out the means of subsistence of the Lakotas and other Plains nations. Even Philip Sheridan, who led many military campaigns against native resistance, admitted late in his career, "We took away their country and their means of support, broke up their mode of living, their habits of life, introduced disease and decay among them, and it was for this and against this that they made war. Could anyone expect less?"[7]

African Americans also ranked among the nation's downtrodden. The Civil War and the Thirteenth Amendment brought about the abolition of slavery, and the postwar Reconstruction period saw the southern black population enjoy a brief moment in the sun with Congress and the army, buoyed by much of northern white public opinion, enforcing black voting and officeholding rights. One state, South Carolina, actually had a black majority in its lower house during these years. Poverty persisted, however, as did the fury of white southerners over being reduced to a state of legal equality with their former slaves—or even inequality, as some former Confederates had their own political privileges temporarily suspended. By 1877, northern white public opinion and the Republican Party in Congress had lost the willpower and dedication to use federal authority against southern white supremacy. The earlier sentiments up north for total victory over slavery had now given way to a desire to get the nation back on track and reconcile differences between North and South. By the 1890s, as the southern economy grew poorer for both black and white, the Jim Crow caste system prevailed. In 1890 Republican Henry Cabot Lodge of Massachusetts introduced a bill in Congress, the Lodge Elections Bill, empowering the federal government to intervene to protect black voting rights in regions where disfranchisement was clearly taking place. The bill did not pass, but southern whites nicknamed it the "Force Bill" and felt indignant at the degree of consideration it had received.[8]

With or without race as a factor, the very nature of labor in the new industrial order made for harsh inequalities. Miners in the Comstock Lode of Nevada labored more than two thousand feet below the surface in fierce heat, inhaling dust particles and noxious gases. Miners everywhere lived in constant danger of disaster. In 1869 and 1870 the Pennsylvania legislature, pressed by labor lobbyists, passed laws establishing safety and ventilation standards for some of the state's anthracite coal mines. It took a fire at the Avondale mine in Luzerne County in the summer of 1869, asphyxiating 109 miners to death, to persuade the lawmakers to tighten the measure and apply it to the entire state. Everywhere, factory workers put in ten- to twelve-hour days and faced the constant danger of losing fingers in machinery with no legal protection or compensation. Workers in the steel mills, the cotton textile mills, the railroad yards, and other industrial settings faced similar hardships. Poor families, es-

Jacob Coxey owned a silica sand quarry and bred expensive race horses. Politically, he belonged to the Greenback Party and then gained prominence in Ohio's Populist Party. Courtesy of Massillon Museum, Massillon, OH.

pecially among the new immigrants, needed the labor of men, women, and children to survive on the prevailing low wages. Managers frequently fired workers for taking part in union organizing, knowing that there were thousands of newcomers from eastern and southern Europe to take their place.[9]

If workers suffered during ostensibly "normal" times, they really knew hardship when depression hit. For three decades in a row, year number three—1873, 1883, and 1893—saw the economy take a sharp nosedive. In each instance, large numbers of workers lost their jobs. Local communities had both municipal and privately run relief operations, but their efforts were far outstripped by the degree of poverty that economic downturns wrought. Moreover, even in times of clear economic crisis, some editors and intellectuals heaped scorn upon the poor and jobless, treating poverty as stemming from moral inadequacy rather than larger systemic causes. When the unemployed traveled long distances on foot or by train in search of work, they acquired the dismissive label of "tramps." During the depression of the 1870s, the *Chicago Tribune* suggested "putting a little strychnine or arsenic in the meat served to tramps" as a means of deterring more of their numbers from coming into a neighborhood. Yale Law School Dean Francis Wayland, in an 1877 conference paper, described the prototypical tramp as a "lazy, shiftless, sauntering or swaggering . . . utterly depraved savage." (Wayland would have similar things to say when a contingent of Coxeyites passed by Yale in 1894.) Some states passed "tramp laws," making it a crime to travel without visible means of support.[10]

Coxey's Commonwealers of 1894 were not the first unemployed laborers to demand government-run public works jobs, but the earlier protesters tended to target city administrations rather than Washington. On December 11, 1873, in the throes of the panic of that year, four thousand persons packed New York's Cooper Institute while thousands more stood outside in the pouring rain to make their grievances known. On the speakers' platform was displayed a bust of George Washington accompanied by a banner that read "The Unemployed Demand Work." Other signs said "When Working Men Begin to Think, Monopoly Begins to Tremble" and "Government Employment, a Remedy for Strikes." Speakers at this rally called for New York's municipal government to provide jobs to the unemployed improving the city's parks, streets, and piers and to use a 100-acre plot of land that had been set aside for military parades to build small and affordable houses for workers. Resolutions drafted that night also suggested that, if the workers' plight remained desperate, workers might have to help themselves to the food and shelter they needed and let the city pay the bill. After all, the resolutions argued, workers had created the nation's wealth and defended it in war, so what they now demanded was not charity, but merely their due. Workers in Boston held a similar rally that night at Faneuil Hall, and in Chicago and Cincinnati workers paraded the streets that month with the slogan "Work or Bread."[11]

In New York, the agitation and the city's efforts to subdue it led to a violent confrontation. One of the leadership cadres in the protest, the Committee of Safety (whose name might conjure up echoes of the most radical phase of the French Revolution of the 1790s), organized a rally at Tompkins Square Park on January 13, 1874, for which some seven thousand persons braved the bitterly cold temperature to show up. Unbeknownst to most in attendance, including many immigrant workers, women, and children, the city had decided to revoke permission for the gathering just the night before. Clashes with police ensued—1,600 uniformed men had been assigned to the square that day—with some protesters fleeing and others putting up a fight. Forty-six of the protesters were in jail by day's end; many others had felt the impact of policemen's clubs on their heads. Some labor leaders and laborite editors observed that the money the city spent on breaking up the rally might better have been spent on creating the public works jobs that the protesters demanded. "When organized labor asks for bread," the *Irish World* angrily noted, "or rather a means to make its bread, you must not offer a stone. Or if you do, it will take the stone only to hurl it back to destroy you."[12]

With few exceptions, the mainstream urban press sided with the police in episodes like this, depicting them as protecting law-abiding citizens from dangerous radicals. Editors of the city papers also showed themselves unsympathetic to the idea of public works projects in times of unemployment. A *New York Graphic* editorial in 1873 suggested that lost jobs would not have affected workers so acutely if they had practiced better thrift: "They want so many of the comforts of life that laying up money is out of the question. . . . A spirit of manly self-reliance is the best friend a workingman can have at any time." Editorials depicted relief, including public works, as penalizing those who had saved up for a rainy day to reward those who had not. Civic and political leaders and much of the urban middle class were in line with this view. In Paterson, New Jersey, taxpayer protests cut short a street repair project designed to help the unemployed.[13]

Meanwhile, for those who still had jobs, labor disputes sometimes turned into out-and-out warfare. In 1877, the fourth year of that decade's depression, a series of pay cuts for workers at the major railroad companies led to the Great Railway Strike, which turned especially fierce in Baltimore, Pittsburgh, and Chicago, causing considerable property damage and leaving scores dead in clashes with federal troops. In the spring of 1886, during another economic slump, a strike along Jay Gould's southwestern lines led to a round of arson and death in East St. Louis, Illinois. On May 4, amid nationwide strikes for the eight-hour day, striking workers in Chicago attacked strikebreakers, and police fired into the crowd, killing four. Local radicals called for a protest rally the following night at Haymarket Square. There, in the midst of an inflammatory speech by one of the organizers, police charged the crowd. Some unknown person then threw a bomb, and a general melee ensued in which at least ten persons died, including several police officers, whom other officers may have shot in the confusion. The eight anarchists who had organized the rally and whose stated ideologies did not preclude the use of homemade bombs (one suspect, in fact, had been seen with one the day before) stood trial for the bomb throwing and the deaths that followed. The trial resulted in convictions and death sentences. (Debate over the defendants' connection with the bomb persists to this day.) Four were executed, one committed suicide in prison, and three survived long enough for John Peter Altgeld to become governor and pardon them.[14]

Whether disaffected workers and radical thinkers posed a big or a small threat to America's economic and political systems, defenders of the status quo felt extremely threatened by them. Many pointed fearfully to the Paris Commune of 1871, where a worker uprising had precipitated a horrific bloodbath, as an example of where "mob rule" could lead. Such worries led the businessmen of Chicago in spring 1874 to respond to the "bread or work" rallies of the unemployed by forming a local National Guard unit, and one of the arrests made at Tompkins Square Park on January 13 was of a German socialist whose offense was carrying the Commune's red flag. A journalist observed of the 1877 railway clashes, "The Commune has risen in its dangerous might, and threatened a deluge of blood."[15]

Events like the Great Railway Strike and the Haymarket affair raised some governmental awareness of workers' privations and grievances but did not result in major reforms. In 1883, a Senate committee traveled from city to city and took 3,000 pages of testimony on labor-management relations. Grover Cleveland, in his first of two stints as president, asked Congress in 1886 to create a permanent arbitration board for labor disputes, noting that "the grasping and needless exactions of employers" and the government's reputation for always taking management's side played a large part in the problem, even while "the laboring men are not always careful to avoid causeless and unjustifiable disturbance." Congress passed only a fraction of Cleveland's desired legislation, allowing for the creation of temporary boards to resolve labor conflicts.[16]

Incidents of violent labor strife persuaded some industrialists that what workers needed was some paternalistic guidance, to keep them mindful of their duties to God and country. George Pullman, pioneer of state-of-the-art dining and sleeping cars for the railroads, built a "model town" not far from Chicago in the late 1870s for employees of his Pullman Palace Car Company with this in mind. Employees paid rent to him, shopped at his stores, and lived their lives under the company's watchful eye. Many worshiped at a Protestant church that he had built, though others set up their own congregations in improvised space. Tourists visiting the town, admiring the beauty of the public spaces, did not go far enough inside to see how cramped and devoid of amenities the workers' tenement units actually were. Americans finally got to see the crack in this utopian veneer when the big Pullman strike broke out in 1894, the same year the Coxeyites marched.[17]

Radicals and Reformers

In all the incidents of protest, including the march of the Coxeyites, conservative critics branded the disaffected workers, or at least their organizers, as *communists* and *anarchists*. These terms, though often used without precision, actually had very precise meanings: they referred to hard-core radicals who viewed capitalism as fundamentally oppressive and illegitimate and who hoped to enlist angry workers to rise up against it and bring it down. Radicals included the German-born Karl Marx and his followers, who envisioned a strong socialist (or communist) state replacing the old order. Anarchists, tutored by the Russian revolutionary Mikhail Bakunin, rejected any form of centralized government and called instead for local workers' collectives to replace the state.

Undeniably, these ideas had vocal agents in the United States as well as in Europe. In the major industrial cities, revolutionary cadres published newspapers and formed worker-based clubs. For a time, the International Workingmen's Association, or First International, which Marx had founded, had its headquarters in New York, though it disbanded in 1876. The Socialist Labor Party came into existence as the standard-bearer of Marxism in 1877, with a founding membership of 2,500. German immigrants dominated both the SLP and the anarchist cadres in Chicago, but the leadership also included some Americans not of German descent. After the execution of Albert Parsons, one of the Haymarket eight, his widow, Lucy Parsons, believed to have been a former slave with African, Mexican, and American Indian blood, stayed active in the anarchist movement.[18]

Even so, American workers generally did not look to socialist or anarchist doctrines to understand their grievances, even when they took part in protest rallies that socialists and anarchists had organized. Radical theory in its pure form, after all, dismissed both religious faith and patriotic loyalty as false consciousness. When members of the labor force spoke out in the language of a belief system critical of industrial capitalism and of their own bosses, it tended to be, not radicalism, but producerism. Producerism lay at the heart of the Coxeyite protests of 1894, as well as of most labor movements in the nineteenth century.

Derived from revolutionary-era theories of republicanism and from Thomas Jefferson's vision of a nation of small farmers and craftsmen, producerism cast economic matters in terms of two groups of people: those who earned their living by *producing* something and those who grew rich living off the producers' labor. In this broad line of thought, the trouble with the new industrial order was that it allowed nonproducers to amass large profits at the expense of those who produced. "The poor unfortunate laborer . . . *produces* all the wealth," a witness representing labor told the traveling Senate Committee on Labor and Education in 1883, "while the men who produce nothing *have* all the wealth." Another concurred: "Jay Gould never earned a great deal, but he owns a terrible lot."[19] In producerist thought, bankers who lent out money to profit from the interest represented the epitome of nonproducers. So did land speculators, those legendary villains who snatched up large tracts of frontier land at low cost to resell for a much higher price after towns and industries had grown up around it, thus keeping it from the industrious farmers who might otherwise have used it to produce something. Also prominent as objects of producerist scorn were the monopolists, or "robber barons," who sat atop powerful, competition-squelching corporations and profited, not by laboring, but by monopolizing the resources. One frequently found lawyers on the nonproducer list as well.

Skilled craft unions—associations of cigar makers, shoemakers, steel puddlers, etc.—strove to remind the public that skilled labor created the nation's wealth. The Knights of Labor, which embodied the labor movement for a time though it was not a union per se, also spoke and acted in the producerist mode. The Knights started out as a fraternal society with secret rituals, founded by a group of garment cutters in Philadelphia and at first holding all of its assemblies there. (The secret rituals fell away in 1881, as the movement became national, largely to avoid bringing Catholic members into conflict with the rules of their church.) As it grew by the mid-1880s to a national organization, the affiliated locals of the "great brotherhood" included both "trade assemblies," organized by specialized skill, and "mixed assemblies," open to skilled and unskilled laborers of every stripe, as well as to merchants and business owners. Indeed, many shopkeepers—especially from small towns—did join, though wage earners always constituted the great majority. But the order singled out five occupational groups, considered idlers and parasites rather than producers and therefore ineligible for membership: land speculators, bankers, professional gamblers, liquor dealers, and lawyers.[20]

The Knights' two key leaders, evangelical Protestant Uriah Stephens (Grand Master Workman from 1871 to 1879) and Irish Catholic Terence Powderly (Stephens's successor through 1893), were known for their disdain for both the wage system and strikes, though Powderly was more of a pragmatist than a purist in these matters. Consistent with the idealized republican model of the master craftsman who owned a small workshop and could set his own prices, the Knights' leadership pursued a strategy of forming cooperatives: stores and manufacturing concerns worked by members of the organization and owned by its locals, as well as one short-lived foray into mining that the central organization attempted. But this idea ran up against several inconvenient realities. For ventures of any complexity, small-scale cooperative proprietorships did not always work. When such a cooperative did succeed, its operators might be tempted to turn it into a profit-making joint stock company and underpay the workers to benefit the stockholders, thus creating the very dragon they had sought to slay. Member support for such ventures had its limits, in any event, and cooperatives found formidable adversaries in the corporations they were trying to compete with.[21]

While the top leaders had their misgivings about strikes, the actual workers and the organizers at the local level generally did not. The Knights' peak membership in 1886 reflected a popular impulse for militant activism, including strikes, rather than for the cooperative movement. It was Knights District Assembly 101 that led the strike against Jay Gould's railroads, and the Knights in Chicago were at the forefront of the eight-hour movement and the strikes that led to the events at Haymarket. The latter episode played a part in the organization's decline, as many among the public incorrectly associated the Knights with the Chicago anarchists. Tensions between the leadership and the members as well as the competitive challenge of the trade union movement also greatly weakened the order. Membership in the Knights peaked at just over 729,000 in 1886, up from 104,000 only a year earlier, then fell, hitting 100,000 in 1890. The organization, however, still existed in 1894, when the Coxeyites marched.[22]

As the Knights of Labor declined, the American Federation of Labor rose.

The AFL consisted of member unions organized by specialized skilled trades, led by German immigrant cigar maker Samuel Gompers. By the last decade of the nineteenth century, the AFL had assumed its position as the leading national labor organization, abandoning, for decades to come, the idea of a coalition between skilled craftsmen and the growing ranks of unskilled industrial labor.

Workers and union organizers in the Gilded Age also took part in direct political action. Numerous "workingmen's" political parties came and went, both before and after the Civil War; indeed, labor candidates ran in many elections in the late 1870s and 1880s. Usually they did not garner large shares of the vote, but there were exceptions. Knights leader Terrence Powderly actually served three terms as mayor of Scranton, Pennsylvania, from 1878 to 1884, elected as the candidate of the Greenback-Labor Party (discussed below). Economic reformer Henry George got a stunning 31 percent of the vote when he ran for mayor of New York in the fall of 1886 on the Union Labor ticket, up against Democrat Abram Hewitt, who won, and a barely known Republican politician named Theodore Roosevelt. Though after the mid-1890s Gompers led the AFL away from partisan activity, especially third parties, he did support the Henry George campaign in 1886.[23]

While labor reformers on third-party tickets had a hard time winning elections, one should not suppose that the larger public held any kind of solid consensus for laissez-faire capitalism. The fact that Henry George's *Progress and Poverty*, published in 1879, and Edward Bellamy's *Looking Backward*, which came out in 1887, sold as well as they did shows that the producerist critique of the new order was garnering some sympathy in middle-class American thought. These works, though not bringing about any massive policy reforms, spawned clubs around the country dedicated to advancing—at least verbally—their particular blueprints for a better tomorrow.

Henry George was paying close attention when the events of the Great Railway Strike of 1877 unfolded, and he wrote *Progress and Poverty* during the two years that followed. As the title implies, the book dealt with the question of why, with all the advancements made in the production and generation of wealth, came such acute privations: Why was there poverty in the midst of plenty? "Some get an infinitely better and easier living," he wrote, "but others find it hard to get a living at all. The 'tramp' comes with the locomotive, and almshouses and prisons are as surely the marks of 'material progress' as are costly dwellings, rich warehouses, and magnificent churches."[24] He found that classical economic theory, radicalism, and the demands of labor agitators all missed the point. For him, the problem boiled down to a basic two-word concept: land monopoly. Labor, in order to produce, needed land. Unfortunately, too much of that land was in the hands of greedy landlords and speculators—the land monopolists—who used that land to reap unearned profits in the form of rent.

This posed a philosophical quandary for George. On the one hand, he opposed all radical schemes that would disrupt land-ownership rights. On the other, he considered the earth's resources to belong to all, and he blamed most of the country's economic evils on the ability of individuals to monopolize land at the expense of others. George's solution was a "single tax" on land, a tax that would increase as the value of the land increased. This would keep the sacred norm of land ownership intact but inhibit individuals from owning any more land than they needed for their own productivity, freeing up millions of acres that other individuals could now own for *their* productivity. He devoted a chapter near the end of the book to describing the sheer utopia that would now result. Most significantly for the urban laboring classes, the new landowning and farming opportunities would draw many workers out of the cities, allowing those who remained to command higher pay. The chain reaction would affect all parts of society, making resources and job opportunities sufficiently abundant as to "eliminate from society the thieves, swindlers, and other classes of criminals who spring from the unequal distribution of wealth." Best of all, this utopian society would be rid of "the great host of lawyers who are now maintained at the expense of producers." (He did not propose to *kill* all the lawyers, as had one Shakespearean character, but merely to redirect their wasted talent toward "higher pursuits.")[25]

Like Henry George, who continued pushing the single-tax plan throughout the 1880s, Edward Bellamy also thought Americans could solve all problems of labor and inequality by developing a more enlightened attitude and restructuring the political economy. The utopia that Bellamy outlined in his 1887 novel might sound like pure socialism to some, but Bellamy took pains to eschew both the word and any encouragement of working-class agitation to bring about the desired ends. Rather, it was the reading and thinking classes whom he hoped to inspire to transform society. He called his philosophy *nationalism*, and the societies that the book spawned around the country called themselves *Nationalist Clubs*.

The protagonist of *Looking Backward*, 30-year-old Bostonian Julian West, writing from the vantage point of the year 2000, recalls how, in 1887, he was both very privileged and very smug about it. In vintage producerist language, he explains at the outset to his readers of 2000 how, back in those unenlightened days, a sum of money that his great-grandfather inherited had lasted and grown sufficiently to make his whole lineage perpetually wealthy.

> The sum had been originally by no means large. It was, in fact, much
> larger now that three generations had been supported upon it in idleness,
> than it was at first. This mystery of use without consumption, of warmth
> without combustion, seems like magic, but was merely an ingenious ap-
> plication of the art now happily lost but carried to great perfection by
> your ancestors, of shifting the burden of one's support on the shoulders
> of others. The man who had accomplished this, and it was the end all
> sought, was said to live on the income of his investments.[26]

Yet the Julian West of 1887 has his problems. Chief among them is insomnia, for which he must sleep each night in an induced trance in a subterranean vault. He awakens one day from this deep sleep, in the home of a Dr. Leete, to discover that the year is now 2000. While he has slept, utopia has dawned.

Julian questions Dr. Leete about what has transpired during these 113 years. He learns of a new labor and economic system in which credit has replaced currency, in which one's occupation is a combined product of individual choice and community need, and in which any undesirable job can be made more desirable merely by shortening the hours. Nobody complains, because everybody can plainly see this system's obvious merits and glories. People no longer even need umbrellas: the new cooperative system has produced a much more effective, all-around sidewalk cover to take their place, and a wall painting where a crowd of people awkwardly maneuver their own individual umbrellas is understood to symbolize all that was wrong with the individual-istic old order. What is more, Julian's host assures him, in the making of this transformation, "there was absolutely no violence. . . . Public opinion had become fully ripe for it, and the whole mass of the people was behind it."[27] In common with Henry George's envisioned world, this utopia has no lawyers.

This book sold well. Obviously, not all readers agreed with the specific remedies Bellamy proposed. But like *Progress and Poverty*, *Looking Backward* spoke to the general sentiment of deploring great poverty amid great progress and of seeing this phenomenon as running contrary to the country's founding principles. In the producerist tradition, Bellamyites packaged their drastic proposals for expansion of governmental power as the mere preservation or restoration of tradition. Bellamy declared in 1890, "We are the true conservative party, because we are devoted to the maintenance of republican institutions against the revolution now being effected by the money power."[28]

Even so, an airtight wall did not always separate the ideological realms. With reformers and radicals sometimes competing for influence and at other times working together to organize rallies, angry workers did not need to agree on every fine point with those who were standing up for them. Moreover, though a broad-based coalition never developed among the different producerist and anticapitalist groups, attempts were certainly made. There were, of course, also voices dismissive of the reformers, such as that of Yale sociologist William Graham Sumner, associated with the theory of social Darwinism, or "survival of the fittest." Sumner and those of his persuasion rejected most blueprints for the government to alter economic inequalities, viewing those inequalities as the necessary price of progress rather than as injustices in need of remedy.[29]

Even amid the rise of mass industry and the problems of urban labor, most Americans still farmed. Farmers, moreover, had no shortage of economic sorrows or of grievances against the corporate world. In the 1870s, farmers in Illinois, Indiana, and other states mostly in the Midwest lobbied through their fraternal organization, the Patrons of Husbandry, also called the Grange, for regulations of the prices charged by the railroads and storage facilities on which they had to depend. Like the Populist movement, which came later, the Granger movement extolled the philosophy that the hardworking and patriotic farmers should not be robbed of a decent living by the monopolistic practices of a greedy corporate world. The Supreme Court let stand state Granger laws that limited the rates grain elevators charged farmers for storage of their surplus. However, it struck down state regulation of railroads that ran through multiple states in 1886, on the grounds that the Constitution reserved the powers of interstate regulations for Congress.[30]

Congress indeed filled that void the very next year with the Interstate Commerce Act of 1887, which outlawed a number of hated practices by the railroad companies and created a new regulatory bureaucracy to oversee them. Three years later, Congress passed the Sherman Antitrust Act of 1890, which outlawed "any combination or conspiracy . . . in restraint of trade or commerce," thus announcing that giant corporate monopolies would be reined in and, when necessary, cut down to size. These acts did not, by any means, revolutionize life overnight for those who had to do business with corporate giants; railroad executives soon dominated the Interstate Commerce Commission, and the Sherman Act in its first decade of existence worked more often in the federal courts against labor unions than corporations. Nonetheless, both acts represented huge symbolic victories for producerist ideology and opened the door for stronger (though still limited) acts in future decades. They also kept Americans talking about a basic question: In good times and bad, what role should government play in American economic life? While many of the specifics changed, this broad question lay persistently at the heart of American politics—and of the march of Coxey's Army in 1894.

Goldbugs and Populists

A question even more central to the political debates of the nineteenth century than the role of government in economic life was the matter of currency. When Coxey called for the federal government to employ the jobless to build and repair roads, part of the plan was to expand the amount of money in circulation by paying the workers with government-issued paper money, a direct challenge to the gold standard, which conservatives held sacred. This fit in with his earlier political activities: in 1877, while still living in Pennsylvania and working as an iron mill engineer, 23-year-old Coxey, believing that scarce currency had caused that decade's depression, organized a local club of the recently formed Greenback Party. This movement represented a fusion of producerist ideology with a very specific monetary theory, one that foreshadowed Coxey's naming his newborn son Legal Tender in 1894, and also the slogan on the banners of his march that year, "Death to Interest on Bonds." The Greenback, or Greenback-Labor, program drew upon the writings of a formerly wealthy merchant who had gone bankrupt in the panic of 1837 and had spent the next two decades theorizing about how to prevent such catastrophes. Consistent with producerist thinkers both before and after him, Edward Kellogg observed critically that a handful of men who did not labor any harder or produce any more than others were amassing great concentrations of wealth. He viewed the power of bankers over interest rates, made possible by use of a scarce metal currency, as a prime culprit in that unfair inequality. In the producerist tradition, he prescribed a remedy: the government, rather than the banks, should control the availability of credit and the amount of currency in circulation. It should do so, he argued, by issuing two key commercial instruments: fiat money, backed by the government's own decrees, and low-interest bonds, which people could purchase with fiat money and, when more advantageous to do so, exchange for that money. The ultimate end of this policy would be to ensure fair monetary compensation to the laborers for the wealth they produced with their labor.[31]

Kellogg died in 1858, three years before the Civil War began. During the Civil War, out of sheer necessity, Congress did something like what Kellogg prescribed, but not exactly: it authorized the issuance of $150 million in paper notes, known as greenbacks, and it allowed specially chartered national banks to purchase interest-bearing bonds from the federal government and to issue notes up to 90 percent of the face value of those bonds, circulating as currency and backed by the bonds, profiting the banks while financing the war. Of this feature, the Greenback movement and Coxey were most sharply critical. Instead of helping the bankers make money through interest rates on scarce currency, the government should make sure there was enough money in circulation to ensure that *workers* made a decent living for their *labor*. "Civil government should guarantee the divine right of every laborer to the results of his toil," the 1880 Greenback platform declared, "thus enabling the producers of wealth to provide themselves with the means for physical comfort, and the facilities for mental, moral and social culture." The platform that year also included some demands that anticipated not only Populism a decade later but also Progressivism in the early twentieth century: an end to western land speculation, regulation of the railroads and public utilities, limits on child labor, safe working conditions in factories, women's suffrage, and a graduated income tax—all this alongside the federally controlled fiat money system implied by the party's name.[32]

Though paper money would eventually triumph in the twentieth century, its enthusiasts made up the least influential faction on the currency question throughout the nineteenth, and the Greenback Party was one among numerous third parties in those years that stimulated debate but gained little long-term traction as parties. In the 1880s and 1890s, the currency question mostly pitted the goldbugs, who wanted the nation's currency limited to the gold supply and all bank notes to be redeemable for gold, against bimetalists, or silverites, who wanted the government to increase the amount of money in circulation by coining silver. Among other effects, expansion meant that those who owed money, including many southern and western farmers, would be able to pay it back more easily because the dollar amount that they owed would have a reduced value. For the same reason, those to whom money was owed—including the whole establishment of bankers and investors—wanted its value kept constant. Silver miners, of course, had their own interest in silver being coined.

Monometalists and bimetalists viewed the issue not just as economics but as fundamental morality. As an academic discipline, the study of political economy was closely intertwined with moral philosophy, sometimes taught by scholarly clergy and understood by many in theological terms. Goldbugs framed the question as one of whether the nation would keep its commitments to its investors by allowing them a secure return on their investments or act as a thief by inflating the currency and causing investments to lose their value. Gold-standard purists also invoked Gresham's Law, which stated that, when two forms of currency circulate and one is being artificially overvalued (in this instance, silver), the overvalued currency will flood the economy and cause inflation, while the undervalued (but more genuinely valuable) currency will flow out of the country or fall into the hands of hoarders. Those who favored expansion of the currency, on the other hand, argued that the gold standard made it easier for the rich to monopolize wealth and resources while others stayed trapped in a cycle of debt and dependency. For them, more money in circulation meant more money in the pockets of farmers and laborers—the nation's *producers*—and relief from oppressive debt burdens. A series of contradictory congressional acts involving silver coinage from 1873 to 1893 reflected this tug-of-war between two intensely committed camps. In keeping with a longstanding American tradition, members of each camp regarded their opponents as representing not just a misguided theory, but a sinister plot.

Unlike the currency debate, social welfare policy per se was not yet a major political issue at the national level, and the Democratic Party had not yet aligned itself with the vision of a strong federal role in social services. Poor relief, as noted, remained a local function in the nineteenth century, with only occasional, sporadic proposals at the federal level. Many took it as an article of faith that the federal government must not put itself into the business of dispensing personal assistance. In 1887, in response to a serious drought in Texas, Congress passed a bill authorizing the Department of Agriculture to distribute $10,000 worth of seeds to farmers in the counties most affected— not a big expenditure even at that era's prices. Democratic President Grover Cleveland vetoed it, declaring, "I do not believe that the power and duty of the General Government ought to be extended to the relief of individual suffering which is in no manner properly related to the public service or benefit. . . . The lesson should be constantly enforced that, though the people support the Government, the Government should not support the people."[33]

This was also not yet the era in which regulation of big business was a partisan issue pitting Democrats against Republicans. Indeed, much of the middle class shared a concern about monopoly. With regard to regulation of corporations, the two landmark acts of the period—the Interstate Commerce Act of 1887 and the Sherman Antitrust Act of 1890—passed Congress with strong bipartisan support and a Republican president's signature on the latter. The two parties did fight over tariffs on imported goods: Should their purpose be merely to raise necessary revenue or also to protect American industries from foreign competition? Republicans in Congress consistently defended higher tariffs to protect industry; Democrats were consistent in verbally claiming to oppose protective tariffs, though not so consistent in voting against them when their corporate constituents demanded otherwise.

On the undesirability of Chinese immigrants, both parties agreed. Congress passed the Chinese Exclusion Act of 1882, prohibiting Chinese laborers (though not merchants) from entering the country. Chinese immigrants to America had few defenders, even in otherwise progressive circles. (The Knights of Labor, racially inclusive in its membership where African Americans were concerned, countenanced several acts of anti-Chinese violence on the West Coast during this time.)[34]

The men who marched with Coxey in 1894 were industrial laborers, but the march had close connections with—was in large part made possible by— the Populist movement, which farmers took a strong hand in building. The People's, or Populist, Party grew out of the multiple Farmers' Alliances of the late 1880s and early 1890s, and Jacob Coxey was a prominent member of that party in Ohio, where it drew stronger support from industrial laborers than in other states. In fact, he ran for Congress on the Populist ticket in late 1894, fresh from the march. Populists nationwide rendered some of the most vital support to the march at spots along the way, while in Washington, Populist politicians serving in Congress gave the strongest defenses, not to Coxey's specific ideas, but to the Commonwealers' right to petition the government in the manner that they did.

The movement came from a number of interrelated struggles. In much of the South, including Texas, farms by the late 1880s grew cotton and little else. A cotton farmer, after spending the year going into debt to the local merchant, had no choice at harvest time but to sell the entire crop at once. Because thousands of other farmers had to do the same thing at the same time, their cotton glutted the international market and drew very low prices. Meanwhile, in 1886 and thereafter, the wheat farmers of Texas, Kansas, and several other southwestern states faced another problem: drought. With the bad harvests came mortgage foreclosure. For the crops that the western farmers did successfully produce, they had to rely on exorbitantly priced railroads to transport them to their buyers. For the affected farmers, this added up to a strong sense of grievance against the banks, the railroads, and the general eastern-based corporate behemoth, all of which they saw as robbing them of the fruits of their labors. President Cleveland's veto of the 1887 Texas seed bill, moreover, confirmed for many that their robbers were running the government.[35]

Not surprisingly, the Farmers' Alliances—brought together by lecturers who went from town to town to organize and recruit—found their greatest base of support in Texas and Kansas. The Southern Alliance, growing out of the Texas movement, was the largest; the Northwestern Alliance represented some of the western states' organizations. There was also a Colored Farmers' Alliance in the South. White Alliances could at times work cooperatively with black groups, but only within the limits of what would not threaten the color line. Black Populists who launched protests or boycotts on their own—which did happen on a number of occasions—were likely to meet with deadly reprisals.[36]

Like the Knights of Labor, the Alliances started out by setting up cooperatives. In 1887 farmers in Texas created the Alliance Exchange to purchase tools and seeds for farmers and to negotiate prices for cotton. For a brief period, the exchange actually sold farmers' cotton on the world market, bypassing the established merchants. It collapsed within a couple of years, however. Having counted on 250,000 members to pay two dollars annual dues (more than many could afford at 1890s price levels), the Alliance did not collect nearly that much. It had also arranged for its more prosperous members to cosign "joint notes" to help needier farmers obtain loans, but it often found banks unwilling to honor these notes. Alliances in other states attempted cooperatives, too, to aid growers of tobacco in North Carolina, citrus fruits in

Florida, and wheat, fruits, and vegetables in California. Though the cooperative strategy did bring one powerful monopoly to its knees—the consortium
of makers of jute bags for cotton—most other such efforts failed.[37]

Frustrations with cooperatives and the continued hardships facing southern and western farmers led Alliance leaders to do what might well have
seemed unthinkable: call upon the federal government to expand its powers.
Indeed, the Alliances by 1889 had drawn up the blueprint for the subtreasury
plan, whereby the federal government would build and operate warehouses
for farmers to store their grain and cotton harvests and would extend low-
interest loans to the farmers, using their stored crops as collateral, thus spar-
ing them from having to sell the whole crop at once at low prices and borrow
money at high interest. Alliances by this time also demanded coinage of silver
and federal ownership of railroad, telegraph, and telephone services, pointing to the postal service as the model for how the national government could
make itself useful by providing essential public services at low rates. Their
proposals represented drastic challenges to laissez faire and dramatic exceptions to the customary fear (especially among southern whites) of a strong
central government, but for the Alliance leaders, these demands represented
the struggle of the nation's true producers to reclaim their government from
the corporate usurpers.[38]

Blending elements of the traditional and the modern, the Alliance movement spawned scores of newspapers, like Charles Macune's *National Economist* and William Peffer's *Kansas Farmer*, that kept farmers abreast of the latest
scientific discoveries related to farming and articulated economic and social
theories on how to improve their lot. The impulse to create a new political party did not come right away, and when it did, not all Alliance leaders
supported it. The Democratic Party, it should be remembered, had a virtual
power monopoly in the South, with many southern whites viewing challenges to the party as a threat to their racial controls. In western states like
Kansas, where the Republican Party dominated, fears arose that a third party
would help the Democrats. For a time, Alliances tried to influence policies
by pressuring mainstream party candidates to endorse their demands. But
when the "yardstick" tactic failed to bring about change, demand arose for a
third party. It began at the state level. In coalition with other reform societies,
Alliances in 1890 created independent parties in Nebraska, Colorado, South
Dakota, and Kansas.[39]

Kansas Populists (as they were soon called) could boast some of the strongest popular support and some of the most colorful characters, and indeed, Kansas was where the new movement made the best showing at the polls that year. Here, Mary Elizabeth Lease purportedly exhorted farmers to "raise less corn and more hell," a brazen expression for a woman to utter at the time (if she actually did). Annie L. Diggs, a journalist seasoned in both the temperance and the women's suffrage campaigns, made her presence known as well. The brothers Henry, Leo, and Cuthbert Vincent, veterans of the Greenback and Union Labor parties, published a bold reformist paper, the *American Nonconformist*. And then there was William A. Peffer, editor of the *Kansas Farmer*, whom the state legislature sent to the U.S. Senate at the end of 1890. Peffer's unusually long flowing beard made him look like a biblical prophet to his admirers and a crackpot to his adversaries; cartoonists had much fun drawing him. Though their state was nowhere near Coxey's route, Peffer, Diggs, and Henry Vincent all played important roles in the 1894 Coxey saga.[40]

The years from 1889 to 1892 saw a flurry of conventions as representatives of white and sometimes black southern and western Alliances, the Knights of Labor, Bellamyite Nationalists, Georgist Single Taxers, and other organizations met to consider the prospects for united political action. In the summer of 1891, rallies throughout the South and West resembled religious revival meetings, with songs, prayers, and rousing speeches. Populists rewrote hymns, singing, for example, "To Beat a Poor Hayseed Like Me" to the tune of "To Save a Poor Sinner Like Me," showing not irreverence for the originals but confidence that God favored their crusade. "Christ himself was the author and President of the first Farmers' Alliance," one orator boldly declared. In the Midwest, especially in Ohio and Illinois, industrial workers even more than farmers helped the new People's Party take shape. By 1892, it was decisively up and running, especially strong in the West and South but also present and commanding attention in much of the rest of the country.[41]

Thus, on the eve of the 1890s depression and the Coxey march, the lines of debate were drawn. What was the proper role of government in the economic lives of ordinary Americans, and what measures should and could be taken to alleviate privation, especially during the recurring economic downturns? Moreover, given that many Americans wanted drastic action taken on behalf of struggling farmers and industrial laborers, how much unity could reform advocates muster, and what would it take to make their demands a reality? These questions clearly stood ready to be put to the test, especially when the country experienced yet another major economic collapse.

2 Hard Times: The Crisis of the 1890s

"THE FRUITS OF THE TOIL OF MILLIONS," Minnesota Populist Ignatius Donnelly told a cheering crowd that included Jacob Coxey at St. Louis in February 1892, "are badly stolen to build up colossal fortunes for a few. . . . From the same prolific womb of governmental injustice we breed the two great classes—paupers and millionaires. The national power to create money is appropriated to enrich bondholders . . . and the supply of currency is purposely abridged to fatten usurers, bankrupt enterprise, and enslave industry." This gathering, convening on Washington's birthday and formally titled the National Industrial Conference, drew large delegations from the major producerist organizations: the National Farmers' Alliance and Industrial Union (NFA&IU), itself the product of multiple mergers within the southern-based movement; the Knights of Labor; the Colored Farmers' Alliance; and several other reform organizations, mostly rural. Frances Willard, president of the Women's Christian Temperance Union, served as vice-president of the conference but did not succeed in getting resolutions for liquor prohibition or women's suffrage passed. Leonidas Polk of North Carolina occupied the top spot.[1]

Coxey, attending as an alternate with the Ohio delegation, had already drawn up a plan for the Secretary of War to issue $500 million in greenbacks for the construction of roads in each county, with workers to be paid $1.50 for an eight-hour day. His Good Roads plan did not receive much attention at St. Louis, but one plank of the platform demanded a national currency "without the use of banking corporations," adding that one means of circulating the currency should be "by payments in discharge of [the government's] obligation for public improvements." Coxey had more influence in Ohio: the People's Party held its state convention that August in Coxey's town of Massillon, and the following year the state party's platform included his complete Good Roads blueprint.[2]

Donnelly's speech at St. Louis became the opening section of the platform that the more formally constituted People's Party convention issued that July at Omaha. Still determined to show themselves the most genuine patriots of all, the Populists opened the convention on the Fourth and attempted, though not successfully, to have exactly 1,776 delegates in attendance. (The count came closer to 1,400.) The Omaha platform listed the demands that had become strict doctrine in Populist ideology: government ownership of the utilities, a graduated income tax, expansion of the currency through issuance of silver at the sixteen-to-one ratio, and an end to land speculation, to importation of contract pauper labor (mainly alluding to the Chinese), and to use of Pinkerton guards against strikers. The platform also expressed support for the eight-hour-day movement and for a Knights-initiated boycott of clothing manufacturers in Rochester, New York. James B. Weaver of Iowa, a former Greenbacker and abolitionist, received the nomination for president, with Confederate Major James G. Field as his running mate.[3]

The reference in the Omaha platform to the Pinkertons was timely. Labor unionists hated Allan Pinkerton, along with his private security agency, for his eager willingness to engage his men as antiunion spies and protectors of strikebreakers. Days before the Omaha convention opened, a conflict at Andrew Carnegie's steel plant in Homestead, Pennsylvania, located along the Monongahela River a few miles up from Pittsburgh, had started to take shape. Two days after the delegates at Omaha issued their Independence Day manifesto, the bloody confrontation at Homestead occurred. Class warfare may not have always dominated American industrial relations, as Marxists would have it, but steelworkers and their allies certainly stood in a state of all-out war against corporate managers and their hired defenders on July 6, 1892, at Homestead.

Andrew Carnegie, who once praised labor unions in theory, had left his plant manager, Henry Clay Frick, in charge of operations and departed for a sojourn at his castle in Scotland. Three years earlier, the strong, AFL-affiliated Amalgamated Association of Iron, Steel, and Tin Workers had won concessions in a strike. Now Frick, determined to break the power of the Amalgamated and to cut production costs with labor-saving machinery, announced pay cuts for the workers when their contract expired in June of 1894. All parties knew that this would lead to a strike, so Frick made the preemptive move of a lockout: he had an eight-foot-high fence built around the compound, and he hired a crew of Pinkerton guards to ensure safe passage for strikebreakers.

Unfortunately for those 300 Pinkerton guards, who arrived on two barges on the Monongahela, there was nobody to ensure *their* safe passage. The plant had almost 4,000 workers, and by day's end their number had more than doubled, swelled by neighboring supporters. The technology of the telegraph allowed unionized workers around the country to register their support as well, as the struggle was all about a powerful corporation defeating a union and rolling back its hard-won gains. Frick's fence stood no chance of staying erect when the angry workers set upon it, and the Pinkerton men, even after they had given up on any objectives beyond going home in one piece, stood little chance of doing even that. Workers and Pinkertons exchanged gunfire in two early-morning rounds. The strikers also made several attempts to set the barges on fire. Finally, labor and Pinkerton leaders negotiated a truce that would allow the Pinkertons to get out, but even then, they had to walk a gauntlet of punches and kicks, incurring the crowd's rage for both the fallen workers and the greater evil that the whole name of Pinkerton represented to the labor movement. Henry Clay Frick did not go unpunished: anarchist Alexander Berkman shot and wounded him on July 23. The union and its member workers lost the battle. Replacement workers still came, protected not by 300 Pinkerton guards, but by 8,000 state militiamen. Carnegie's plant at Homestead was now nonunion. The force of strikebreakers included numerous African Americans, which should have come as no surprise to a union that had kept its membership, and thus the skilled workforce at Homestead, all white.[4]

Compared with uprisings and suppressions elsewhere in the world, the number of deaths on July 6—estimated at seven striking workers and three Pinkerton guards—was small. Still, the Homestead lockout, like the events of 1877 and 1886, showed the ever-present threat of larger-scale civil warfare between organized labor, on one side, and management, with hired guards and federal troops, on the other. To conservatives, this meant the need for stronger policing to protect law and order, as well as better citizenship lessons for workers and tougher immigration policies, since any disrespect for corporate property surely came about from the influence of foreign radicals. Radicals, of course, viewed even the most militant of worker uprisings as baby steps toward waging the true war against capitalism itself. In between those two poles were voices of reform, calls for greater legal protection of workers' rights and needs in the unequal bargaining relationship with the corporate world.

This was, of course, a presidential election year. Grover Cleveland and his Democratic Party agreed with the Populists on one point: protective tariffs bestowed unfair advantages and powers on American corporations. Their platform, after a lengthy opening section condemning the Lodge Elections (or "Force") Bill, declared that "the Federal Government has no constitutional power to impose and collect tariff duties, except for the purpose of revenue only, and we demand that the collection of such taxes shall be limited to the necessities of the Government when honestly and economically administered." It then called the recently passed and highly protective McKinley Tariff "the culminating atrocity of class legislation." The 1892 Republican platform, in stark contrast, explicitly called for protective tariffs on "all imports coming into competition with the products of American labor" and blasted the Democrats for their "efforts . . . to destroy our tariff laws by piecemeal." On currency, both parties endorsed bimetalism, with the Democrats holding more strongly to the need for more silver and denouncing the Sherman Silver Purchase Act of 1890, a compromise measure that had authorized the coinage of far lesser amounts than they were demanding, as "a cowardly makeshift." On this issue, the platform and the candidate clashed: Cleveland, an uncompromising goldbug, hated the Sherman Act for the opposite reason.[5]

In the 1892 elections, the People's Party ticket of Weaver and Field received 8.5 percent of the popular vote and the electoral votes of five western states. Three Populists achieved the state governorship—significantly, all in the West: Sylvester Pennoyer in Oregon, Lorenzo Lewelling in Kansas, and Davis Waite in Colorado. The results also sent ten Populists to the House of Representatives and, after state legislatures had voted, five to the Senate, including William V. Allen of Nebraska and William M. Stewart of Nevada, joining Peffer from Kansas. With seats in state legislatures included in the count, 1,500 members of the People's Party won office that year. Even so, in Washington only one party could claim serious victory: the Democrats, who now controlled both chambers of Congress and the presidency. House Democrats quickly elected Charles F. Crisp of Georgia their speaker. In Texas, the southern state with the strongest Populist movement, incumbent governor Jim Stephen Hogg survived a Populist challenge to win reelection.[6]

The 1892 race made Cleveland the only chief executive in American history to win reelection for a nonconsecutive term. (He had lost to Republican Benjamin Harrison in 1888.) He stepped back into office amid great optimism, at least among political leaders. Harrison, in his last message to Congress, told the legislators, "There has never been a time in our history when work was so abundant, or when wages were as high, whether measured by the currency in which they are paid, or by their power to supply the necessaries and comforts of life." Cleveland affirmed that perception in his inaugural address on March 4. He also sounded a note of caution: "The strong man who in the confidence of sturdy health courts the sternest activities of life and rejoices in the hardihood of constant labor may still have lurking near his vitals the unheeded disease that dooms him to sudden collapse." The next part foreshadowed his unsympathetic response to Coxey's demands of the following year. The "unheeded disease," he made clear, came from efforts to dethrone the gold standard. Cleveland subscribed firmly to Gresham's Law insofar as currency was concerned. Soon thereafter, he reaffirmed the same opposition to new federal social welfare functions that he had expressed in his first term. "The lessons of paternalism ought to be unlearned and the better lesson taught that while the people should patriotically and cheerfully support their Government[,] its functions do not include the support of the people."[7]

The Collapse of Hardihood

Even before Cleveland took office, disaster began to strike. First the Philadelphia and Reading Railroad went bankrupt, on February 26, 1893. The stock market noted the news by suffering the largest single-day decline to date. The other shoe dropped on May 5, just after the much celebrated World's Fair in Chicago opened, with the collapse of the National Cordage Company. The market fell again. A chain reaction had begun, and it now accelerated with a vengeance. Banks began calling in loans and refusing to make new ones. Then a series of railroads failed, including the Northern Pacific and the Union

Pacific. This put them into government receivership, meaning that they continued to operate with their managers in charge, but under the immediate supervision of federal courts. (This idiosyncratic feature affected the course of some Coxey-related events the following year.) By the end of 1893, 500 banks and 16,000 businesses had closed their doors, and unemployment had reached 20 percent. It went considerably higher in some industrial centers, notably Chicago.[8]

Among the many small businessmen whose ventures failed in 1893 was one Robert Walker of Youngstown, Ohio. His disaster wrought at least as big a crisis for a friend of his named William McKinley. Walker had helped McKinley through law school with loans and later contributed to his political campaigns. McKinley had shown his gratitude by casually cosigning loans for Walker which, as he apparently did not know, approached $100,000 and which, in any event, he did not expect would come back and bite him. As it happened, these loans bit him at a most inopportune time: during his term as governor of Ohio. He learned of this sudden liability in February 1893, on the eve of the larger national crisis. Though he did not want to take charity, a group of his close associates, led by political handler and friend Mark Hanna, began an earnest fundraising drive, drawing large contributions from the wealthy and small ones from ordinary well-wishers. While some feared that McKinley's reputation would suffer from this, McKinley received far more sympathy for his plight and admiration for his generosity than any scorn.[9]

On magazine pages and in public forums, the familiar debates resounded over whom to blame for the crash and what to do to reverse it, with one set of thinkers blaming Wall Street greed and treachery, and other voices holding that the government had failed to inspire investor confidence. President Cleveland, believing that the Sherman Silver Purchase Act of 1890 had caused the collapse and that its repeal would repair it, called Congress into special session in August. In his message opening that session, he declared that the nation's economy had all the conditions conducive to growth and prosperity and that the nation's current "unfortunate financial plight" was "principally chargeable to Congressional legislation touching the purchase and coinage of silver by the General Government." Contention in Congress came largely along lines of East versus West. The House, which the larger states of the Northeast controlled, complied with Cleveland's wishes before the end of the month. Debate lasted longer in the Senate, where the less populated, newly admitted western states held more sway. Populist Senator William M.

Stewart of Nevada remarked scornfully, "He calls Congress together now that he has a panic on hand, which he helped to make, to see if they will be more obedient to his imperial will." Not just Populists, but also nearly all western members of Congress opposed Cleveland on this. Even so, the act of repeal narrowly passed the Senate. Cleveland signed it on the first of November.[10]

Cleveland and his treasury secretary, John G. Carlisle, then turned to a closely related issue. Here again, the administration acted on the premise that economic recovery required the continued confidence of both local and foreign investors in the American productive sector. Conventional wisdom held that, come what might, the U.S. government must always have $100 million of gold in its treasury, and be able to meet demands for redemption of paper certificates from the surplus over that amount, to maintain its place in the global economic community. The first year of depression had seen the gold reserves fall into the danger zone, and in January 1894 the gold reserves stood at the intolerable level of $62 million (though the government had ample currency in other forms at its disposal). Cleveland and Carlisle moved to stanch this hemorrhage by issuing a bond sale to bring in gold. When sales disappointed, Carlisle solicited the help of New York bankers in the sale of these government securities, leading Senator Peffer to declare, "In the face of idleness, destitution, hunger and desperation . . . the President is compelled to sell the people's credit to appease the clamor of these misers of Wall Street." Carlisle turned to the bankers for an even larger-scale gold drive the following year, after the gold reserves had dipped down again, rescuing the gold standard at considerable profit to J. P. Morgan and his colleagues.[11]

Cleveland further showed his dedication to a single currency by vetoing a bill in April 1894 under which the treasury would have coined the unused silver that still sat in its vaults (known as the *seigneuriage*). At the same time that Cleveland antagonized silverites, he also scored low with Republicans for attempting to lower protective tariffs and with Democrats for not succeeding.[12]

While political leaders in Washington haggled over how to revive the economy, state and local governments as well as private charities and labor organizations addressed the human face of the crisis. Boston put some unemployed men to work cutting wood, Detroit provided public garden space for the poor to grow food, and a number of cities found jobs for the jobless working in sewers and maintaining streets and parks. Chicago, under labor-friendly Mayor Carter Harrison, employed 1,400 job seekers on the city's drainage canal and 2,000 more tending to the quality of the streets—one of Harrison's last official acts before his assassination. Numerous cities and towns around the country accelerated plans for road, park, sewer, and water projects in order to alleviate joblessness. Legislatures in some western states, where hard times had begun much earlier in the form of drought, appropriated money to grant seed, coal, and other supplies to farmers, while some counties in North Dakota provided relief by not collecting taxes in 1894.[13]

Alongside local government efforts, voluntary organizations such as churches and labor unions provided meals and cash relief, and more formal charity societies stepped up their efforts. Churches ran soup kitchens, and private merchants underwrote supplies of beef, bread, and coal for distribution to the poor. A group of volunteers in Boston raised supplies and ran a small network of low-priced restaurants and food pantries staffed by unemployed persons. Newspapers, including the *New York Tribune* and the *Buffalo Courier*, set up emergency funds to distribute supplies. Charity organizations also set up "wayfarers' lodges" for the homeless. Labor organizations, when they could afford it, ran their own relief programs. Cigar makers could get unemployment benefits from their union, and a shoe-lasters' union in Lynn, Massachusetts, supplied five-cent meal tickets to members out of work. In various cities, the affluent ran charity balls, and working people donated portions of their wages for poor relief. Yet even in times of desperate unemployment and hunger, voices in the reform community called on dispensers of aid to distinguish between the deserving and the undeserving poor, between workmen out of work and "professional tramps," and to make the relief onerous enough that the recipients would never prefer it over bona fide work or internalize socialistic values from it.[14]

In the year before the Coxeyites marched to demand that the federal government create jobs for the unemployed, the familiar debate raged over whether state and local governments had any such obligation. On August 20, 1893, an estimated eighty or ninety delegates representing about thirty labor organizations met at the International Labor Exchange on East Tenth Street in New York. Samuel Gompers, who called the convention, delivered the keynote address. He blamed the distress of the unemployed squarely on "the wealth possessors of this country," and he sounded the call for help.

> But how can we get relief? Why, this city can begin almost immediately to build its rapid transit road, improve its streets, sewerage, wharfage and docks. This State can improve its roadways and deepen the Erie Canal.

This national Government should build the Nicaragua Canal [referring to the intended waterway that ended up running through Panama], should dredge the Mississippi and make one navigable ship canal from it to the Peninsula of Michigan.

Theologian William T. Stead, visiting from England, remarked similarly in his scathing book-length critique of neglect of the poor, *If Christ Came to Chicago*: "There is no excuse for a city like Chicago in which the elementary necessities of sanitation and of street cleaning are so poorly attended to for refusing to provide a labor test for the tramp. . . . There is work enough to be done." In Boston, Edward Bellamy proposed a system of state-run workshops for the unemployed, while the unabashed socialist organizer Morrison I. Swift, who later led a contingent to Washington, visited the State House in February with perhaps as many as 2,000 unemployed men, petitioning for jobs in state-operated farms and factories.[15]

As in earlier decades, the idea that governments should create projects especially to provide jobs, or favor those most needful of employment in their hiring for public projects, drew many cold rebuffs. "It is plain," the *New York Times* told its readers, "that the municipal officers have no authority to make work for anybody, any more than they have to give away the money of the taxpayers in charity." What the city *should* do, the paper further opined, and which would have the *incidental* effect of modestly relieving the distress, was accelerate the public works projects already intended, so as to make good use of the cheaper labor now available, without "forming a select and favored class of workmen," presumably referring to those most desperate for work. The following month, at the Syracuse State Fair, New York's governor, Roswell P. Flower, responded to Gompers' proposals. Flower admitted in this speech that many were suffering in this financial panic, though he hastened to add—incorrectly—that conditions were already starting to improve. He expressed great admiration for private charity efforts and assured listeners of his intent to proceed with construction projects already planned. Even so, he rejected the idea of calling a special legislative session, invoking reasoning previously heard from the lips of President Cleveland. "In America the people support the government; it is not the province of the government to support the people. Once recognize that the government must supply public work for the unemployed, and there will be no end of official paternalism."[16]

While city governments and private charities made what efforts they could or would, the intensity of the crisis again far exceeded the available relief. Newspapers reported sad stories of struggling families facing eviction, and occasionally of extreme cases like that of twelve Italian immigrant families in a Long Island City tenement house, starving and freezing and about to lose their home. Depression drove a number of people to desperate measures. Some stole to feed their families; others threw rocks at windows in plain sight of police in hopes of spending the night in a warm jail cell. Some young women resorted to prostitution to eat. Many traveled in search of work. Westbound trains filled with unemployed Texans expecting more job opportunities in California whizzed past similarly filled eastbound trains of the unemployed from California hoping to find conditions better in San Antonio and El Paso. Some of these passengers had transportation subsidies from charities like the Salvation Army; others stowed away in freight cars. Chicago reported hundreds of men from the West stepping off the trains daily in quest of work, in a city whose unemployed population was already large from the number of unemployed workers who had built the World's Fair facilities. At one point, police started guarding the stations to block any more vagrants from disembarking.[17]

The same defenders of the status quo who opposed reform viewed the high number of roving unemployed persons as a danger to the rest of the population. Before there was a Coxey's Army, the metaphor of an army gained some usage as connoting potential invaders by whom the middle class might feel menaced. "Some communities," an observer told a researcher, "when the hard times came this winter, and the army of the unemployed swept through the streets, were panic stricken, the inhabitants fortified themselves behind soup-houses, and threw loaves of bread out upon the besiegers; naturally the siege continued." New York's Governor Flower, in that same September speech, also remarked that "men and women, deprived of work, see destitution and misery confronting them. . . . How vast this army of unemployed is nobody can accurately estimate."[18]

Police departments of different cities had different policies for the homeless unemployed. Some allowed them to sleep in police stations, while others would only accommodate them in the jails as arrested vagrants. (The slang term *vagged* popularly meant arrested for vagrancy.) Reverend Stead observed more than a thousand people sleeping in Chicago's city hall. When jobless men, finding no employment opportunities in their own locales and unable to keep their homes, traveled to other cities and states in hopes of finding something better, they found themselves referred to as tramps, and their presence considered a "tramp" problem rather than a "jobs" problem. Police in Buffalo, New York, enforced the state's tramp act harshly, arresting 4,716 persons for vagrancy in 1894, more than double the number in any one of the previous three years. Some authorities were more sympathetic. Kansas's Populist Governor Lewelling, recalling his own days as a tramp back in 1865, declared the vagrancy laws unconstitutional and ordered police not to molest the homeless.[19]

The employed had their problems, too. The first year of depression did not see a substantial increase in strike activity, but workers in many industries experienced wage cuts. Among them were the employees of the Pullman Palace Car Company, many of whom lived in George Pullman's much-celebrated model town. When the pay cuts came in the winter of 1893–94, the workers did not rebel right away, but five men, including one Eugene V. Debs, got together in Chicago in June 1893 and formed the American Railway Union, which took up the Pullman workers' cause the following year with a massive strike and boycott.[20] The late winter and spring of 1894 saw a rash of miners' strikes. The gold miners of Cripple Creek, Colorado, began their action in February.[21] Two months later, while Coxey's Commonweal made its way through Pennsylvania and then Maryland, the United Mine Workers of America, led by Coxey's friend John McBride, launched a nationwide strike of bituminous coal miners. The gold miners at Cripple Creek achieved their objective, helped by the anomaly of a sympathetic governor; management prevailed in the coal strike, as was the case when the Pullman conflict boiled over that summer.

Chicago, 1893

Chicago saw much activity in the first year of depression. At the time the panic hit, the city was hosting the World's Fair, with exhibits of cultures, ideas, and technological wonders, including the first Ferris wheel, colorful electric lights, washing machines, moving pictures, moving sidewalks, electric chairs perfect for executing criminals, an early version of the fax machine, and electric boats to ferry visitors around along the fairground's specially designed canals. The fair made the city a magnet for all manner of notables and also for many laborers, who suddenly became indigent when the fair ended. All this

The depression hit at a time of national triumph, as millions were flocking to the World's Fair in Chicago. Here, the new technology of electric lights helps visitors enjoy the sights in the Grand Court by night. LC-USZ62-97300, Library of Congress, Washington, DC.

ensured for the Windy City a loud chorus, or perhaps cacophony, of political voices.

During the first three days of August, the American Bimetallic League held its convention there, culminating in a massive rally at Lake Front Park. Many big names attended, including Populist and other silverite lawmakers, governors, and intellectuals. Mayor Harrison, himself a silverite, delivered a warm welcome address. Again, in keeping with political traditions, keynote speaker Thomas M. Paterson, editor of the *Rocky Mountain News*, made it out to be "a life and death struggle" and opined that "if this country is to remain the land of the free—if it is to remain a country where government by the people is to continue—they must win and they will have only won when the money of the constitution has been restored by bimetallic coinage."[22] (Goldbugs considered the issue just as weighty, with the future of civilization itself riding on the gold standard.) Opposition to monometalism united the delegates, but they did not all agree on whether silver or greenbacks should supplement gold. The gathering took place, of course, precisely while Congress was deliberating over Cleveland's demand for a complete return to the gold standard. Jacob Coxey was at that Chicago convention, advocating for paper money. Observing the glitter of the fair side by side with the misery of the unemployed on Chicago's streets, Coxey saw an immediate connection between all this and the Good Roads project that was not happening.[23]

Lake Front Park had fast become a meeting place for both the unemployed and the orators who sought to enlist them for political crusades. Here Coxey made the acquaintance of a Californian named Carl Browne. Browne, 44 at the time, had already had an eclectic career as a journalist, political agitator, patent medicine salesman, carnival barker, and sketch artist. Just a few years earlier he had stood trial and been acquitted for extortion, and prior to that he had served as secretary to Denis Kearney, organizer of the California Workingmen's Party and leader of a virulent crusade against Chinese immigrant workers. (As noted, labor activism and racism against the Chinese frequently coincided.) Along with Lewis C. Fry, a western Coxeyite commander in 1894, Browne had once organized a march of the unemployed to Sacramento. Now, according to Browne's own account, the San Francisco *City Argus* had dispatched him for an extended sojourn at the Chicago World's Fair to write stories and also to take part in the Wild and Woolly West exhibit, sporting his Buffalo Bill attire.[24]

Browne remained in Chicago into the fall, participating in much of the rallying activity at the lakefront and regaling audiences with his speeches on the evils of Wall Street, illustrated with his colorful canvass cartoons and diagrams. He apparently mingled with two other personages who later figured into the Coxey story: A. P. B. Bozarro (or whatever the real name of this man of so many aliases may have been) and Honoré Jaxon. Exactly what Bozarro did is as unclear as his name, other than that he and Browne were among those who shouted opinions to the crowds. According to Henry Vincent's official history of the Coxey saga, Mayor Harrison, who found the city's radicals a constant irritant, called Browne into his office and admonished him to leave town. Purportedly Browne did so—long enough at least to visit his new friend in Ohio—but returned to Chicago incognito not long afterward.[25]

Honoré Jaxon had taken an even more intriguing path to the city. As recently as 1885 he had served as secretary to Canadian Métis aboriginal activist Louis Riel and, after a rebellion against the Canadian government, had narrowly escaped being executed alongside Riel (who did not escape). After

Carl Browne, a far more colorful character than Coxey, could be found lecturing crowds at Lake Front Park in Chicago in the summer of 1893. Courtesy of Massillon Museum, Massillon, OH.

his move to Chicago, he managed to convince not only himself and his contemporaries but also later generations of authors on the Coxey affair that he had Indian blood himself. (He had none. He was born in Toronto shortly after his parents migrated from England.) In Chicago, he ran a fairly successful sidewalk construction business until he became too busy with his political activities to keep up the work. He secured a spot as the Métis nations' representative, though a Métis only in his imagination, at the World's Fair.

That fall, in an office he rented in the *Chicago Tribune* building right next to the office of the paper's owner, Mayor Harrison, Jaxon hosted a gathering of anarchists. For the occasion, he set up a big tepee in the office and decorated it with tomahawks, buffalo robes, and other such ornaments. Lucy Parsons, widow of executed Haymarket defendant Albert Parsons, took part.[26]

A number of rallies and conventions centering on the rights of workers and the plight of the unemployed occurred that summer and fall in Chicago, with appearances by Samuel Gompers, Henry George, William T. Stead, and local reformer Henry Demarest Lloyd, who had recently published his critique of monopoly capitalism, *Wealth against Commonwealth*. Meanwhile, the World's Fair lasted through October. On the last day, October 28, Mayor Harrison delivered a triumphal oration, boasting of the glory of the fair and of the city that hosted it. One would not know from the speech that the country was in crisis. "I intend to live for more than half a century," he declared, "and at the end of that half-century London will be trembling lest Chicago should surpass it, and New York will say, 'Let it go to the metropolis of America.' It is but a little while when I expect to get on a magnificent steamer at Chicago's wharf and go to a suburb,—New Orleans, the Crescent City of the globe. Mr. Mayor of Omaha, we will take you in as a suburb. We are not narrow-minded. Our heart is as broad as the prairies that surround us."[27] Harrison did not live for another half century, or even another half day. It was still possible in 1893 for a stranger with a gun in his pocket to knock at the door of a big city's chief executive and gain entry. That evening, one Eugene Prendergast, a crazed and disgruntled office seeker, paid him a visit and shot him.[28]

The American Federation of Labor held its convention in Chicago that December. One definitely sensed from this gathering and others that American workers were losing patience with laissez-faire capitalism. As part of the movement to unite the industrial workers with the Populists and move the coalition decidedly leftward, Thomas J. Morgan, Chicago-based head of the International Machinists Union, who also belonged to the Socialist Labor Party, introduced a draft of a "Political Programme" for the AFL. Much of it echoed the Populists' Omaha Platform, though minus the subtreasury demand, but Plank 10 of Morgan's document provocatively called for public ownership of the means of production and distribution. The convention deferred formal action on it till the following year but called upon its member unions to weigh in on the program at their own conventions. The convention's own platform did, however, include a call for government ownership of the railroads and telegraphs and a resolution declaring that "the right to work is the right to life, that to deny one is to deny the other, that when the private employer cannot or will not give work, the municipality, State, or nation must."[29]

In addition, on John McBride's initiative, that 1893 AFL convention, like the Ohio Populists that year, made a platform plank out of the Good Roads plan, calling upon Congress to issue $500 million in greenbacks, at a rate of $20 million per month, for the payment of unemployed workers under the supervision of qualified engineers for the building and repair of the nation's roads.[30] Clearly, some people were listening to Jacob Coxey.

3 Petition in Boots

EARLY IN MARCH OF 1894, CHARLES H. DENNIS, managing editor of the *Chicago Record*, summoned a young reporter named Ray Stannard Baker, later a prominent journalist and author, to his office. Baker's next assignment, his boss informed him, would take him to a little-known town in Ohio. "There is a queer chap down there in Massillon named Coxey who is getting up an army of the unemployed to march on Washington. He is going to demand legislation to cure all the ills of the nation. We hear that he is getting a good deal of support. Go down there and see what it all amounts to." With this commission came a starting expense account of $100, significant money for that time.[1]

So Baker traveled by train to Massillon, a fair-sized town not far from Canton, whose local coal- and steel-producing industries were suffering the downturn. After a horse and buggy ride over some of the muddiest roads he had ever seen, he arrived at a large farmhouse. There he found Coxey and Browne, seated at a dining table covered with "a huge pile of letters, telegrams, and newspapers." Jacob Coxey did not look revolutionary to Baker, but rather "mild-looking and of medium size, with rounding shoulders, an oily face, a straw-colored moustache, and gold-bowed spectacles." Carl Browne, however, "was too good to be true. He was strongly built with a heavy moustache, and a beard with two spirals. He wore a leather coat fringed around the shoulders and sleeves. A row of buttons down the front were shining silver dollars. Cavalry boots, tight-fitting, well polished, came to his knees." Coxey told his visitor, in earnest, that they expected 20,000 marchers to depart with them on Easter Sunday and present their demands to Congress on the first of May. Browne broke in to correct that number: it would come closer to 100,000.[2]

Meanwhile, in Pittsburgh, a Secret Service spy named Matthew F. Griffin followed these developments in stoic anticipation. He knew that some agents with a proven talent for appearing down-and-out would be detailed to infiltrate this band, should it materialize, and that he had shown this ability in previous missions. He thus guessed that, before long, he would be one of the men tramping through the elements hoping for a square meal, a prospect he did not exactly relish. The Secret Service functions to protect the treasury as well as the president, and a march into Washington by a band of 100,000 penniless, desperate men—or even a small fraction of that number—conjured up a menace to both those sacred entities.[3]

As noted, for two years Coxey had already been promoting the idea of a federally funded Good Roads project to put the unemployed to work. However, one key component of the idea, which remained the trademark of his economic vision to the day he died, had come to him more recently—in a dream at midnight on New Year's Eve, he later recalled. Given that government, at all levels, sold interest-bearing bonds to finance its operations and that the ultimate beneficiaries of those bonds were the bankers, the solution suddenly seemed simple. State and local governments should be able to issue non-interest-bearing bonds, representing up to half the assessed value of property within their jurisdiction, for the federal government to buy. The federal government should buy those bonds for 99 percent of their face value, allowing a 1 percent discount to cover legitimate costs of the transaction. The federal government should make that purchase, not with gold or even silver, but with printed fiat money, backed solely by its own authority. The local borrower should have twenty-five years to pay it off, 4 percent at a time, interest free. With that money, Coxey argued, state and local governments could render badly needed repairs to the roads and provide badly needed jobs to the unemployed. Armed with this fine-tuned version of his Good Roads plan, Coxey and Browne had spent much of January 1894 lobbying city councils in Massillon, Akron, and Youngstown to start issuing such bonds to sell, and lobbying Congress to pass legislation to buy them. The lack of interest in noninterest bonds moved them to consider a march, a "petition in boots."[4]

Browne's estimate of 100,000 men in the interview with Baker should not have surprised Coxey too much, because he had used that figure himself in the press release he floated in late January, in which he exuded confidence that the good townsfolk along the way would feed the men. The national press responded by producing short blurbs with mocking headlines. On January 28, the *New York Times* announced, "Look Out for 'Em Congressmen! Here's Mr. Coxey, Coming 100,000 Strong to Do Wonderous Things," while the *Washington Post* that same day burnished the headline "Candidate for an Asylum: The Crazy Idea of a Wealthy Resident of Massillon, Ohio."[5] Yet even these curmudgeonly dailies conceded that Coxey appeared to have a real plan, with, if nothing else, serious determination and serious money behind it. In case anybody should doubt the importance Coxey gave to his monetary theories, when his wife Henrietta gave birth to a boy several weeks before the march began, they named him Legal Tender Coxey. From the start, Coxey and Browne had the arrival date set for May 1, "May Day," which laborites of all stripes recognized as an International Workers' Day.

At first glance, naming the organization the Commonweal of Christ might have suggested the same evangelical Protestant orientation that some of the other movements were associated with. Actually, though, Browne identified with that sect of spiritualism known as Theosophy, or rather, his own creative adaptation of it. According to Browne's personal gospel, the souls of living people were composites from a reservoir of the souls of people who had once trodden the earth. Conveniently, he could thus theorize that he and Coxey had strong traces of the spirits of both Jesus Christ and former president Andrew Jackson in their own souls. (Jackson was still remembered for his 1833 war on the Second Bank of the United States, a symbol of financial privilege.) How else, Browne reasoned, could he and Coxey have found each other, formed such affection for each other, and worked so harmoniously to formulate the Good Roads plan? They had a division of labor, moreover: Browne considered himself the Cerebellum of Christ, and Coxey his Cerebrum. Browne's cosmology had direct practical applications: he believed that the arrival of this army in Washington would make for such a thick concentration of Christ's soul in one place that Congress would have to fulfill the words "Thy Kingdom come,

MRS. HENRIETTA COXEY AND LEGAL TENDER

Jacob Coxey's second wife, Henrietta, supported her husband to the end. Several weeks before the march began, the couple named their newborn son Legal Tender Coxey. Courtesy of Massillon Museum, Massillon, OH.

they will be done on earth as it is in heaven" by passing the Good Roads bill. Some, including members of Coxey's family who considered the whole scheme crazy, perceived Browne as the instigator of the march. A few even wondered if he had Coxey under some kind of supernatural spell.[6] Baker's editor captured the perception of many when he instructed the novice newsman, "Don't put Browne too much in evidence as the hero of the plot is Coxey, though he seems to be rather a puppet in Brown's [sic] hands."[7]

Before long, most of the newspaper-reading public knew that Ohio had a town called Massillon with an apparently eccentric resident named Coxey. In Massillon, meanwhile, curious spectators and a growing corps of reporters watched as Coxey and Browne prepared to set forth. A special telegraph room was set up at one of the local hotels to accommodate the unusual flurry of press activity. Browne busily spruced up his panorama wagon and designed banners for display, with slogans including "The Farmer Leads for He Feeds" and "Workingmen Want Work Not Charity." The pair led camp meetings, with

Coxey appearing more as the studied intellectual and Browne the animated fanatic. The press monitored the arrivals. In the days leading up to March 25, the scheduled departure date, the number of ready marchers remained low, but a handful of colorful personages gave the reporters material to write about. Most prominently, of course, stood Browne, in attire suggestive of frontier legends like Davy Crockett and Daniel Boone. Browne's associate from Chicago, Bozarro, arrived on March 19. Tall, slender, spiffily dressed with a precisely trimmed moustache, limping with a cane, he was introduced to the watching throng at the town square that night with the tantalizing name "The Great Unknown." (The Chicago reporters knew who the Unknown was, as he had graced their city with his bravado that previous year, but they played along. Browne later came to wish Bozarro were unknown to *him*.)[8]

Other popular characters included "Oklahoma Sam," a young cowboy named Samuel Pfrimmer, whom Coxey had employed on one of his horse farms and whose trick-riding skills captivated the young children who came around to watch; "Weary Bill" Iler, who would drive the panorama wagon, oversee the food supply, and reputedly fall asleep at every possible chance; Douglas McCallum, a social critic from Chicago, author of the allegorical political book *Dogs and Fleas, by One of the Dogs*, which he hoped to sell to curious spectators; and J. M. "Cyclone" Kirkland, whom Baker described as "a little man who wore a battered silk hat." An amateur physician, though nearly blind, and an astrologer, Kirkland claimed that the stars had foretold this march as the greatest movement in the world's history. He was at the time working on an epic poem modeled after Homer's *Odyssey*, and he read passages of it to whoever would listen. Populist editor Henry Vincent arrived on Saturday to lead a portion of the army while writing its official history. Honoré J. Jaxon, the notorious labor activist from Chicago who claimed "half-breed" Indian status, arrived on the eve of the march as well.[9]

Baker, according to his later recollection, did not take any of Coxey and Browne's plans seriously, but he dutifully telegraphed dispatches on their doings to his editor in Chicago. Then one afternoon Coxey passed him with the latest sack of mail from the local post office and told him with a big smile, "We're beginning to hear from your articles in Chicago." "It struck me all in a heap," Baker wrote in his 1945 memoir. "So I was helping to launch this crazy enterprise!" Letters did indeed pour in. So did checks—some real, some fake. Eugene Prendergast wrote Coxey with his regrets that he could not take part in the march, as he now sat on Death Row for the assassination of Chi-

cago's Mayor Harrison. As the starting date drew nearer, more correspon-
dents from major city papers began arriving in Massillon. Even now, with few
actual unemployed men in sight to do the marching, many wondered if the
march of Coxey's Army would actually happen. A cartoon in the *Pittsburgh
Post* depicted a procession of Coxey, Browne, the Goddess of Peace, an array
of reporters, and one disheveled tramp. According to Baker's memoir, Charlie
Seymour of the *Chicago Herald*, reflecting the press corps' fear of letting down
its readers, even suggested that the reporters might pay a dollar apiece out of
their own expense accounts to a hundred local circus roustabouts, seasonally
unemployed and camped nearby, to help get the march started. Nothing came
of the idea—nor did it turn out to be necessary.[10]

During the afternoon preceding Easter Sunday, reporters and other observers of the goings-on at the grounds of the Massillon Gun Club could not
deny that the Coxey scheme had something to it. True, they did not expect
the army to approach 100,000, or even 1,000, any time soon, but they did see
about 100 men already present, with reliable reports of more on their way,
as tents were pitched and wagons made ready. The reporter for the unsympathetic *Washington Post* overestimated the force that would depart the next
day at 500. The *Post* reporter conceded that the men on the grounds had thus
far "shown no inclination to be unruly" and quoted from an official order by
Browne that "all members of the army except those assigned to special duty
are expected to remain in camp so that if any depredations are committed
they cannot be laid to the Commonweal." In case anyone disobeyed that order, the mayor of Massillon had his local forces on special alert.[11]

"Everybody March!"

Early Easter morning, a bugle sounded in the camp. The men, camped by
the Tuscarawas River, arose, washed, and ate breakfast. By eight o'clock they
were in formation for an hour-long drill session led by Bozarro (Smith, or the
Great Unknown, to them). Around nine, Browne preached a sermon. Then,
while an estimated 10,000 spectators crowded the streets of Massillon to see
what they could, the men lined up to begin the march of Coxey's Army. At
eleven thirty, Bozarro bellowed "Everybody march!"[12]

Jasper Johnson, an African American man from West Virginia, led the way
as the flag bearer. His bulldog, Bunker Hill, walked faithfully by his side. The
seven-piece marching band, conducted by John J. Thayer, followed. Browne

rode his stallion behind them, wearing his usual buckskin attire, with his white necktie added for the occasion. Nearby rode Bozarro, bedecked in white and blue with a bright red saddle, continuing to yell orders, and Oklahoma Sam, on his bay nag. Coxey's own fancy carriage, called a phaeton, followed, with an African American man driving Coxey, his wife, her sister, and three-week-old Legal Tender Coxey. (These last three only accompanied Coxey for the short ride out of Massillon.) Then came the unemployed men themselves. Available estimates of that starting lineup at Massillon (not counting staff, who rode) range from seventy-five to a little over a hundred. Among them walked a few undercover agents sent by the Pittsburgh police and some number of federal Secret Service agents, all to provide some advance reconnaissance on these indigent travelers who would soon grace their respective cities with a visit. Matthew Griffin, still in Pittsburgh, felt relieved at not having been assigned to this mission.[13]

Behind the marchers rode the wagons, including the commissary wagon carrying the food and other supplies and Browne's celebrated panorama wagon, with his banners and diagrams. "Weary Bill" Iler drove the team of horses that carried this all-important vehicle. Coxey had wanted the procession to begin with the Goddess of Peace, adorned in white atop a horse of the same color, but his first wife, thinking him totally insane, had adamantly forbidden their 17-year-old daughter, Mamie, to fill that role. The press had reported the day before the march began that Coxey had recruited a local young woman named Anna (or Annie) Bauhart, to do the job, but the actual procession out of Massillon ended up without a goddess. (Mamie later disobeyed her mother and caught up with the army in Washington.) Coxey's 18-year-old son, Jesse, made the full trip with his father.[14]

In spite of Coxey's reluctance to use the word *army* or identify himself as a *general* (which did not stop the public and the press from referring to him as "General Coxey" till the day he died), the organization of the Commonweal employed military terms and procedures to an enormous extent. Browne's associate Bozarro (the Great Unknown / Smith) drew upon his own military background, though nobody ever got clear exactly what that background was, to provide strict discipline and drill. Browne divided the Commonweal into groups of five, each having its own group marshal, and had them federated into companies and communes, the latter representing units that joined the march along the way and maintained a degree of internal autonomy. In theory a company or commune would have 100 men, five companies would form a

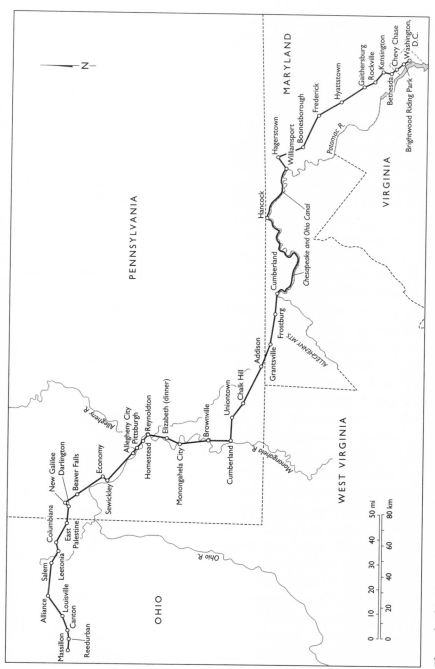

Through Ohio, Pennsylvania, and Maryland, the Commonweal of Christ trekked to deliver a "petition in boots" to Washington. How many men actually made the journey from start to finish is unknown. Courtesy of Bill Nelson.

community, and two communities would constitute a canton. The reality of the numbers did not entirely sustain this structure, but the Commonweal had groups, companies, and communes at every step, and leadership always ran along hierarchical lines. The men wore badges decorated with Browne's drawings. The wagons also displayed banners of his artwork, including a composite portrait of Browne and Christ.[15]

The men marched that first day through howling wind and snowfall. Reporters noted that most had no overcoats or gloves. They stopped at Reedurban, nourished themselves with salmon sandwiches from sympathetic townspeople, and completed the nine-mile stretch from Massillon to Canton around four in the afternoon. Their ranks increased along the way, more than 200 sleeping at Canton, though only about eighty men set out the next day. (The size of the army continued to rise and fall from new recruits and desertions.) The men set up camp in a lot adjacent to the town's workhouse, pitching a tent that, though large, could not accommodate all of them. Coxey and Browne named the night's lodgings Camp Lexington. (Every stop received some purposeful name.) Sympathizers brought dry straw for the men to lie on. As happened for most of the march, locals brought them dinner. The men found that night's offering especially palatable, with 200 boiled hams and a bounty of potatoes and baked beans; many subsequent meals featured just bacon and hardtack, and many were small. After dinner, the leaders lectured the curious throng from the panorama wagon. At nightfall, while the Commonwealers found what comfort they could on the ground under the big traveling tent, Coxey and Browne departed and slept in the genuine comfort of a hotel, as did the reporters. According to Coxey's publicist, Henry Vincent, a citizens' committee at Canton hoped to launch a nationwide fund drive for Coxey's Army, considering the men at least as worthy of such aid as Governor McKinley had been the previous year.[16]

Monday morning, day number two, Coxey had mail. Populist Senator William M. Stewart of Nevada had written him a letter, undertaking to persuade him of the folly of this march. After declaring (as Coxey agreed) that a "soulless despot" called money held the reins of power in Washington, he urged Coxey to realize that the way to alter this unfortunate state of affairs was to campaign in earnest for Populist victories through the ballot boxes in November. He sought to warn Coxey against "the folly of marching an unarmed multitude against the modern appliances of war under the control of a soulless money trust." While the Commonwealers waited at the camp, Coxey read the letter and composed his reply. He reaffirmed his resolve, as well as his faith in the peace-loving citizenry along the route. Then, noting Senator Stewart's good record in defense of silver, he admonished his admonisher not to align himself with the gold forces by disparaging this movement. The press printed both letters in full.[17]

The men marched that Monday from Canton, along a crude thoroughfare called the Washington Trail, to Louisville, Ohio. They encountered this town's mayor, absurdly standing guard over the town's brewery with his shotgun. They christened the night's sleeping site Camp Peffer in honor of the Populist Senator from Kansas who had sponsored Coxey's bills in Congress. Soon the mayor, realizing that he had misjudged this pack of visitors, invited them to sleep in the town hall. The Coxeyites always gave three cheers for such locals who showed them kindness. A few Coxeyites visited the local saloon that night, leading to some tensions with a man who accused them of stealing his watch; after some questioning from the mayor, the incident passed.[18]

The march through the Ohio countryside continued, passing farmhouses with big red barns and chickens strutting through the yards. The chickens were safe from harm, at least from the Commonwealers, who had strict orders not to touch them. From Louisville the next day the petitioners in boots trudged to Alliance, where they camped at the local fairgrounds under the name of Camp Bunker Hill. Here the press had some entertainment to report: a mysterious veiled woman, reputedly the wife of the Great Unknown, joined them. Her veil, some observed, covered a black eye. She had reportedly told a hotel chambermaid that she had gotten this injury from a child carelessly throwing a piece of furniture at her, an explanation not everyone believed. Browne, sensitive to any hint of scandal, made sure she did not travel anywhere near the marchers.[19]

March 28 it was on to Salem, on the most miserable stretch of road yet. As they walked in parallel with the tracks of the Pennsylvania Railroad, some hopped rides on passing freight trains, a practice that would grow more difficult the following month. Along the way, at Beloit, a pack of adolescent boys waited for them, all ready to pelt them with snowballs, but upon seeing how weary and forlorn the men looked, the youths took pity and refrained. (In some other spots that day, the marchers were not so lucky.) The Commonweal got a warm reception at Salem and, courtesy of the mayor, two warm indoor halls in which to sleep. They named that night's quarters in honor of Kansas Populist Annie L. Diggs, one of their staunchest allies. They also picked up a

The Coxeyites, somewhere between Massillon and Washington. LC-USZ62-52081, Library of Congress, Washington, DC.

new bugler, "Tooting" Charley. (Their first bugler had fallen by the wayside around the second day.) Thursday, proceeding through a raging snowstorm, they stopped at the mining town of Leetonia to enjoy a meal courtesy of sympathetic townspeople, and slept at Camp Trenton in Columbiana.[20]

Coxey, as much a busy man of affairs now as before, left the marching route several times between Easter Sunday and May Day for business trips. While the woman with the veil was intriguing the reporters at Alliance Tuesday night, Coxey was en route to Chicago to oversee the sale of several of his horses at a stockyard auction. To his chagrin, the sale had taken place without him and had netted less than he would have accepted. He had other horse-related problems as well: he had contracted for the purchase of a stallion named Acolyte at the huge price of $40,000 but had only paid $16,000. According to reports in the press, the seller was now attempting to repossess the animal. How the principals resolved this matter is unclear, but Coxey rejoined the Commonweal late Thursday afternoon, March 29, as the contingent approached Columbiana.[21]

During the lunch stop at Leetonia, Browne gave a speech to the crowd that provided the traveling press with a new sobriquet. "The powers that control and enslave us are greatly scared. They have sent the representatives of a capitalistic press to dog our footsteps and wreck us if they can. I can go nowhere now but that I am followed by forty argus-eyed demons of hell, eager to catch any sentence that will condemn us."[22] Instantly, the journalists adopted that epithet as the formal name of their social club and elected J. R. Caldwell of the *New York Herald* as Arch Demon Number 1 of the A.E.D.H. *New York World* reporter W. P. Babcock provided the order with a song:

> Forty demons marching on,
> Every demon has a horn.
> Drunk at night, and drunk at morn,
> Now we're here, and now we're gone.[23]

Browne eventually found his own sense of humor on the subject.

The "argus-eyed demons" actually played an interesting role in the whole affair. Before the Commonweal's journey had even begun, the editors of the *Washington Post* counseled that, while "this preposterous Ohio crank, Coxey" was not exactly breaking any laws, his plans represented "a grave offense against morals and humanity." Thus, they opined, "it is about time to stop laughing at Coxey and to consider whether there may not be some way of preventing his wickedness and folly."[24] These pious words notwithstanding, the *Washington Post* and countless other papers nationwide, far from preventing Coxey's wickedness and folly, gave his effort an enormous boost by constantly writing about it. Elaborate front-page articles chronicled these pilgrims' progress as well as the simultaneous adventures of the other contingents—the bands setting out from Oakland, Los Angeles, Butte, Chicago, and numerous other spots—who hoped to join Coxey at the endpoint. The coverage also made clear that, for the most part, the Commonwealers held themselves to strict rules of conduct and enjoyed massive, though by no means unanimous, support in communities along the way.[25]

The reporters traveling with the Coxeyites numbered about a dozen at the outset; more joined them as it grew clearer that the Commonweal really would reach the capital. Four telegraph operators and one lineman traveled with the press corps. In spots that had telegraph poles but no office, the lineman had to climb a pole and splice into the wire for a connection. The telegraph operators busily transmitted the reporters' stories in dots and dashes, in time for readers to enjoy the following morning. For as slow and limited as the telegraph and the print newspaper might seem in an age of YouTube and Twitter, for their own time they served quite effectively, allowing Americans to feel close to the action as it unfolded. All through April, front-page news stories culled the latest from the Coxey march, replete with vivid descriptions of the eccentrics, the latest from the other groups out west—including some train heists—and the police preparations in Washington.

The labor and Populist press gave much more sympathetic coverage, reflecting the mindset of their constituents. Local divisions of the AFL, the Knights of Labor, and the People's Party followed the march eagerly and played a role in coordinating support along the way. Members of the AFL-affiliated Central Labor Council in Richmond, Indiana, cheered them with a song to the tune of "Marching through Georgia."

> We are marching to the Capital, three hundred thousand strong,
> With live petitions in our boots to urge our cause along,
> And when we kick our congressmen, they'll feel there's something wrong,
> As we go marching with Coxey.
>
> Hurrah! Hurrah! For the unemployed's appeal!
> Hurrah! Hurrah! For the marching commonweal!
> Drive the lobbies from the senate,
> Stop the trust and combine steal,
> For we are marching with Coxey.

Samuel Gompers, according to his memoirs, never wholeheartedly endorsed the Good Roads plan but nonetheless admired the enterprise and took an ongoing interest in its progress. African American papers also treated the movement with favor.[26]

Pennsylvania

Friday, March 30, the Commonwealers walked through more springlike conditions: a fresh swath of dandelions adorned the picturesque country landscape. (The worst weather still awaited them.) They slept that night at Camp Gompers in the small pottery and mining town of East Palestine, Ohio. Here, a fierce difference of opinion arose between Bunker Hill, the mascot of the color bearer Jasper Johnson, and a dog belonging to a nearby farmer, with the latter canine reportedly losing an ear in the encounter. The next day they crossed the state line into Pennsylvania. Stopping for lunch at Darlington, the Coxeyites saluted the former old stone schoolhouse (now a railway depot) where abolitionist warrior John Brown had once studied. They slept Saturday night in the indoor and outdoor spaces of an old stove factory in New Galilee, which they named Camp Marion Butler, for the president of the National Farmers' Alliance from North Carolina. The Commonwealers were decidedly filthy Sunday morning, from their night on the damp dirt floor; before they could hear the usual Sunday service led by Browne, with his customary blend of Christianity, reincarnation, and monetary theory and with bugle tunes provided by "Tooting" Charley, they were compelled to cleanse themselves in a nearby stream, which locals had presciently nicknamed the River Jordan.[27]

The Commonwealers marched onward and slept at Beaver Falls Sunday night, calling the spot Camp Valley Forge. Monday, April 2, afforded them the longest single-day trek yet, walking alongside the Beaver River, with steep hills on both sides. They made a lunch stop in Economy, a town settled largely by Germans and Dutch, notable for the mostly brick houses adorned with grape vines, an old Dutch Reformed Church, and vast orchard land surrounding the town. Much of the population of Economy belonged to the Harmony Society, a community of celibate religious devotees. One of their leaders, trustee John S. Duss, ensured a warm welcome and a good meal for the Commonwealers, and Coxey thanked him by naming that night's encampment at Sewickley for him. Some in the region revered Duss, while others wrote him off as a crank, which of course gave him some common ground with Coxey.[28]

In numerous spots, tens of thousands came out to cheer. As they moved from town to town, the army picked up new unemployed marchers. "Cyclone" Kirkland did much of the recruiting, philosophizing with the men in the process. To one newcomer with the first name of Peter, Kirkland said, "Peter, Peter—that's a good name. You've heard of Peter the Great and Peter the Apostle. You may sometime be Peter the Great. Try." When morale sagged, he made use of another of his talents and organized a glee club. He reportedly woke up the whole camp one night crying out that he saw a big wheel turning in the sky.[29]

At Rochester, Pennsylvania, young working women from a glass factory watched them pass by in admiration, some charmed by the brass buttons on Coxey's coat. Not all towns were equally welcoming, though. The level of enthusiasm generally correlated with the degree to which either the Populist Party or unionized labor prevailed in the population. At East Palestine, it was said that the town had only two Populists and one of them was sick with the mumps.[30] They found New Galilee dominated by churches that abhorred Browne's reincarnation theories. Beaver Falls, a town overflowing with Populists and laborites, where committees and clubs had spent the previous two weeks preparing for their arrival, welcomed them with great fanfare and five tons of provisions. At Sewickley the Coxeyites received a chilly reception when they first arrived, being afforded a camp but not a dinner by the locals. Police, apparently fearful of marauding, guarded the camp to prevent anyone from leaving. One woman there, according to the *Pittsburgh Press*, "saw [Carl Browne's] sacrilegious banner and said that the author of it should be making shoes in some penitentiary." Tuesday morning the townsfolk, having apparently mellowed after seeing how peacefully the men camped for the night, fed them breakfast.[31]

Beyond Sewickley lay Allegheny City and Pittsburgh, a pair of cities dense with iron and steel mills, glassworks, and oil refineries. (The two cities later merged.) Here the approach of the Coxeyites aroused both the greatest enthusiasm from disaffected laborers and, precisely because of this, the greatest apprehension among the defenders of order. Coxey visited the city several days in advance, making use of both his merchant and Populist connections there. The Pittsburgh area, like most metropolitan regions in times of depression, had serious tensions with its own workforce, with many of the employed on strike and the unemployed demanding assistance. Coxey's arrival on April 3 coincided with the city's announcement that its relief fund had run out and the local public works projects in the city parks had come to an end. Striking coal miners also excited public fears: an angry mob had already murdered Henry Clay Frick's chief engineer, Joseph H. Paddock, leading to several shootings and to mass arrests by Fayette County Sheriff William H. Wilhelm and his posse. Fearing the arrival of the Coxeyites as a catalyst for further combustion, area authorities hoped to move them along as expeditiously as possible.[32]

Several days before their arrival in Pittsburgh, Matthew Griffin received orders from Washington to stop shaving and get out his old clothes. He had not escaped a tour of duty with Coxey's Army after all.[33]

Spectators came out in particularly large numbers for this stretch between Sewickley and the steel city. Schools delayed their opening the morning of April 3 so that teachers and pupils could watch Coxey's Army pass by. Before

At several spots along the way, teachers brought schoolchildren to watch as the increasingly famous Coxeyites passed through their towns. LC-USZ62-93731, Ray Stannard Baker Collection, Library of Congress, Washington, DC.

the Commonweal had even stopped at Bellevue for lunch, a delegation of Pittsburgh detectives met the marchers and inspected them to see if they recognized any notorious felons. At Bellevue, a contingent of cyclists showed up to give a welcoming escort: their organization, the League of American Wheelmen, had applauded Coxey's campaign for improved roads right along. Around three o'clock that Tuesday afternoon, Coxey's Army made its much-anticipated entrance into Allegheny City. The march became a full-fledged parade, with even some of the city's high officials extending hospitality to the visitors. Somewhere between 150 and 200 Commonwealers, led by Coxey, Browne, and the ever-popular Oklahoma Sam, on horseback, marched behind several times as many local unionists, Populists, wheelmen, and prominent police and fire officials riding on horseback and in ornate carriages.

As everybody prepared to stride through the Wood's Run section of Allegheny City to the appointed camping site at a baseball park, the route grew progressively thicker with cheering spectators, some bearing provisions. Some men also stood by with bundles of belongings, apparently ready to enlist. Here, however, the riders and marchers encountered a roadblock. Allegheny City police, fearing mayhem if the marchers took that central route, had decided to redirect them to the back roads, away from the awaiting throngs. A number of men of Iron Molders' Union Number 14, part of the labor contingent positioned near the head of the procession, began fighting the police, but their respected leader, James Shipman, whose local activism dated back to the Greenback Labor Party, ordered them to acquiesce, in the interests of ensuring that no deaths would result. The rerouting disappointed several thousand spectators, including those who had brought food, which they now had to lug to Allegheny City's Exposition Park to donate to the Commonweal.

Once the Coxeyites had set up camp in Exposition Park, the police sealed it off, preventing the men from going out even to buy much-needed supplies. The manager of the local Palace Theatre had intended to invite them to see that night's show as guests of the house, but the city quashed this idea. The men slept that night on uncushioned ground under an annoying drizzle. Police arrested twenty-eight men for vagrancy when they attempted to leave the camp that night; the local court initially sentenced them to thirty days in the workhouse but the next day ordered them released and escorted to the city line. Browne, as part of the meticulous effort to show the leadership's good faith, announced that he would discharge any Commonwealer who sought to venture out.

Coxey's Army stayed put at Exposition Park on Wednesday, April 4, a day that saw the arrest and discharge of more men attempting to flee. The Commonweal also brought in new recruits that day. One identified himself as William J. Murphy, or Willie. Browne issued the man a badge, a dish, and a cup, all of which he could wear while walking, and assigned him to Company E as Soldier 32. Browne admonished the scruffy-looking newcomer to shave, assuring him that the Commonweal had barbers who would gladly assist him. Agent Griffin's education on how to be a good Commonwealer had begun.[34]

The Commonweal leaders spoke at two rallies, one in the afternoon at the Monongahela Wharf, where the sheer weight of the pressing crowd smashed a wheel of Coxey's phaeton, and the second that night at city hall. Those attending the nighttime gathering issued resolutions thanking the Pittsburgh Police for their courtesy, while saying thanks-for-nothing to their Allegheny City counterparts. While camped at Allegheny City, Coxey received an invitation from the proprietor of a dime museum in Pittsburgh to take a hiatus from the army and spend a week or so as one of the exhibits. Coxey declined. When he learned that Kirkland, Iler, and Johnson had accepted this invitation, he booted all three (or four, if one counts Johnson's dog Bunker Hill) from the Commonweal of Christ, declaring, "We will have no dime museum freaks in this aggregation."[35]

One final disagreement with local authorities occurred at Exposition Park that morning, Thursday, April 5. Jesse Coxey wanted to take the commissary wagon around the city to collect donations, but the police would not allow the wagon to leave the park until the entire contingent was ready to leave. The co-chairs of the local committee interceded, and the police relented. Finally, Coxey's Army departed. Escorted by 50 policemen and 500 supporters, including a fife-and-drum corps, the jobless marchers crossed Union Bridge into Pittsburgh proper, where enthusiastic crowds and watchful police stood in large numbers. They marched up Fifth Avenue, passing the Eden Musée, where those three newly discharged men stood sadly and watched them pass by, and the Jones and Laughlin steelworks, where workers stood outside and cheered. Generous donations of food and clothing continued to come their way.[36]

Ahead lay Homestead, where the showdown between striking steelworkers and Pinkerton guards had occurred two years earlier. The Commonwealers received a tumultuous heroes' welcome, complete with the serenade of a steel workers' band. The men bathed in the Monongahela, and the size of the army more than doubled with new recruits. Many of the new marchers— Polish, Hungarian, and Slavic steelworkers who spoke limited English—enrolled as the Pittsburgh Commune (though most of these recruits do not appear to have marched all the way to Washington). Interestingly, one Alexander Childs, nephew of the aforementioned Mr. Frick and relative of some other moneyed notables, joined the Commonweal here as commissary officer. They camped in a structure known as Fred Schulman's Ice House, renamed Camp Homestead for the night.[37]

From Homestead, Coxey's Army walked to Reynoldton, near McKeesport, and called their Friday night lodging Camp J. Edd Leslie to honor one of their prominent local welcomers. Saturday, April 7, they proceeded toward Monongahela City, stopping for dinner at Elizabeth and sleeping that night at Camp Brandywine. At the following night's destination, Brownsville, the men had expected to sleep at the outdoor Camp Chicago but then learned

that the town councils of Brownsville and Bridgeport had made a pair of indoor halls available to them. From Brownsville to Cumberland, the Coxeyites walked along the National Road, an early-nineteenth-century venture of
which Coxey would have approved. For parts of it, the solid clay substance
made walking easier, though other parts needed serious repair. Along the
route, they passed the remains of the inns and stage houses that had once
lodged many travelers and their horses and resounded with the conviviality
of ale-drinking men, before the railroads rendered the road obsolete for long
journeys. Old log houses, with big stone exterior chimneys, and more newly
built barns, with iron ornaments called cupolas on the rooftops, also lined
this stretch. Curious townsfolk, though in smaller numbers, came out to view
the passing spectacle.[38]

The Commonweal reached Uniontown Monday night and pitched the
tents in a baseball field, which became Camp Lincoln. While dinner cooked,
the three men whom Coxey had exiled for posing at the dime museum—
"Cyclone" Kirkland, "Weary Bill" Iler, and Jasper Johnson (Bunker Hill still
by his side)—arrived at the camp entreating readmission. A cadre of officers
led by Browne (Coxey was away on one of his frequent business trips) turned
them down. "Dark clouds are tumbling in the east," reporters heard Kirkland
announce after hearing the verdict. "The blood of Mars is dripping on Coxey.
The war is on. Is it a cyclone or is it a misguided hand? We shall see." He
threatened to make trouble by organizing a "Counterwheel." Even so, little
was heard from that trio (or quartet) after this.[39]

Kirkland did claim credit for one vengeful deed: conjuring up a fierce
storm of heavy rain and wind followed by snow, which kept the Commonweal stranded at Uniontown all day Tuesday. Browne made clear to the men
that the next stretch would be especially difficult and that if anybody felt inclined to drop out, now was the time. Some took his advice and did just that.
The men were about to travel through the Blue Ridge Mountains, moonshine
country, where towns were sparse and the locals—their stone houses displaying squirrel tails and raccoon skins—decidedly unfriendly to the likes of
them. The storm still pounded on Wednesday morning, but the leaders were
determined to make the scheduled arrival date of May 1 in Washington. Thus
they set out, hiking six miles over mud, slush, and snow. They slept that night
in an abandoned colonial mansion at Chalk Hill (Camp Brownfield), surrounded by a foot of snow. Browne issued a formal commendation to the men
that night: "You have demonstrated . . . that you are not the lazy and vicious

class that some of the newspapers brand you. . . . When you reach the other side of the mountains your names will go on the scroll of same. Like Henry V. said to his men after the battle of Agincourt, your names will be as familiar as household words."[40]

The morning of Friday the thirteenth, while preparing to depart from Camp Thomas Jefferson at Addison, the Coxeyites saw a sheriff and his posse approaching. They reacted with displeasure at first, until they learned that this delegation had come, not to harass them, but to protect them from the hostility of the local populace, many of whom craved a confrontation and had all the whiskey it took to fuel their resolve.[41] That afternoon, the men enjoyed the good luck of reaching the state line. To salute their new state of passage, band leader Thayer played "Maryland, My Maryland" on his cornet, with a braying mule providing backup vocals. They slept at Grantsville (Camp Ulysses S. Grant) that night, then proceeded to Frostburg on Saturday.

Rifts and Reconciliations in Maryland

As Secret Service agent Griffin, alias Murphy, assimilated himself into the Coxeyite ranks, a sharp-looking young man among them attracted his attention by expressing some doubts about the value of peaceful petitions. Because "soulless capitalists" owned Washington, the young man had opined to Griffin, "the only way of waking them up is to blow up the whole damned works." When Griffin inquired as to what he meant by the works, the man replied, "The Capitol, the White House, Congress, everything." Later in the trek, in a gathering of Coxeyites and spectators, the same man got up and spoke. "I believe in bettering the condition of the workingman," he announced. "That can't be done by talk. There's only one way to do it." He then restated what that method was. His fellows resoundingly booed him from the stage, but Griffin noted "a few scattering hand claps."[42]

Griffin also observed early on that many in the ranks profoundly disliked Carl Browne. Moreover, both Bozarro, once Browne's bosom buddy from Chicago, and Coxey's 18-year-old son, Jesse, had come to feel that Marshal Browne must go. The press gleefully reported the tensions between Browne and Bozarro (whom they still called "the Unknown" and "Smith"), for instance, Bozarro yelling at Browne one day, "I found you on your uppers in Chicago. I picked you out of the mud." On Saturday, April 14, the day the men awoke at Camp Ulysses S. Grant in the Amish town of Grantville, Maryland, and had

For three days Coxey's Army was a navy, as the Commonwealers and the press corps sailed on three barges down the Chesapeake and Ohio Canal from Cumberland to Williamsport, Maryland. LC-USZ62-92477, Library of Congress, Washington, DC.

to ascend the 2,850-foot, thirteen-mile slope of the Big Savage Mountain, the tensions boiled over. Coxey was off on another business trip. The showdown ostensibly began when Browne rebuked the Great Unknown for taking a food break in front of the marchers, but according to Griffin's account, the men, in cooperation with Bozarro and Jesse, had already planned the mutiny. Shortly after the run-in over the eating, Browne ordered the marchers to stop so that he could address a group of onlookers about his monetary theories, a recurring practice the marchers found increasingly tiresome. This led to a war of commands between Browne, yelling "Commonweal, halt!" and Bozarro, in concert with Jesse Coxey, countering "Commonweal, forward march!" Bozarro called for a voice vote between himself and Browne, with the Unknown calling Browne a "leather-coated polecat" and Browne calling his former friend a Pinkerton spy, the deadliest of accusations at that time. The marchers, following the plan, aligned themselves with the Unknown.[43]

After first trying to commandeer the provision wagons, Browne took possession of Coxey's empty phaeton and sped off with it. He did not get far, however, because one of the two horses died under the added strain. The main procession came upon the spectacle of Browne sitting at the roadside looking utterly desolate and bereft. Bozarro, reclaiming control of Coxey's phaeton, courteously returned Browne's own horse to him. The Commonwealers camped that night in Frostburg, naming the site for Confederate General Robert E. Lee, with "Smith" as their sole leadership figure. Meanwhile, the *Washington Post* told its readers, "This evening Browne has been wildly telegraphing all points to reach Mr. Coxey."[44]

Mr. Coxey arrived at the camp at Frostburg at four that following morning, April 15, covered with mud after a hasty all-night carriage ride. He met first with Browne, then with Bozarro, then announced to the men at breakfast that, no matter how many of them (and it was a huge majority) favored the Unknown over Browne, Browne was to stay and the Unknown was to go. Browne and Bozarro had one last shouting and shoving match, with Bozarro again bitterly attempting to remind his former friend of all he had done for him back in Chicago, whereupon Coxey intervened and decisively sent the exile on his way. He also exiled his disobedient son, though the prodigal repented not long after and was restored to his father's grace.[45]

Browne soon explained to reporters that Bozarro had both good and bad spirits in him from the reservoir of souls and that his evil spirits had unfortunately come to dominate. After this, Browne somewhat eased up with his dictatorial tendencies, and the tensions subsided. In any case, one saw clearly now if not before that Coxey viewed Christ's Commonweal, not as a democracy, but as one of his proprietorships. He alone would decide who shared the command with him. Bozarro, though out of the Commonweal, did not disappear from the story. Along with Alexander "Cheek" Childs (Frick's nephew), he took to running ahead of the army and representing himself as collecting donations for them, to fund his breakaway contingent, which reached as many as twenty-three men at one point.[46]

A pair of new recruits met the men at Frostburg, eager to enlist. When one of them said that he had worked as a telegraph lineman, the recruiter gave him a pair of spurs and instructed him to climb the nearest telegraph pole. The man passed the test flawlessly, and he and his friend gained admittance to the Commonweal. Coxey's Army now had two more spies, this pair courtesy of Major William G. Moore and the capital city's Metropolitan Police.[47]

From Frostburg, the men next trekked downhill to Cumberland. They stayed there at Camp Victory the following day, Monday, April 16, enticed with a donation of $100 from a local electric railway company that was making good money from bringing curious customers to visit the camp. (Monday was also Coxey's 40th birthday.) As they did in a number of other spots as well, the Coxeyites played a baseball game with locals; they also needed much of the day to perform maintenance tasks on their tents and wagons.

Then, in the two days and nights that followed, came a change of routine that afforded the men a reprieve from walking. In the hot sun, before a large and curious audience, the men dismantled the wagons and loaded them, their horses, their personal belongings, and themselves onto two canal boats that normally hauled coal, *A. Greenless* and *Benjamin Vaughn*, for which Coxey had negotiated bargain fares, for a ride down the Chesapeake and Ohio Canal. A third boat, normally called *Mertonville* but temporarily renamed *Flying Demon*, carried the press. Ray Stannard Baker, who had eaten well for most of the trip, noted in a letter to his father that he endured three days "subsisting on greasy eatables."[48] Baker also gave his readers a vivid description of the view from the boat.

> The canal runs through a picturesque country. High brown hills, streaked with strata of sand rocks, are on one side, and a hundred yards away on the other runs the Potomac, hemmed in on the farther shore by irregular cliffs coated with firs and jack pines. It was perfect spring weather. The apple and cherry trees around the little mountain houses were white with blossoms. Dandelions and hepatica sprinkled the grassy canal banks.[49]

They stopped off at Hancock Wednesday evening for dinner and a round of speeches. Had Coxey and his army arrived a little earlier than they did, they might have met a man calling himself James Mason waiting by the dock to join the Commonweal. Before that could happen, Sheriff Wilhelm from Fayette County, Pennsylvania, caught up and arrested him for his alleged role in the Paddock murder.[50]

The canal trip ended at 6 a.m. on Thursday, April 19. The Coxeyites and the "argus-eyed demons of hell" disembarked near Williamsport, Maryland, and set up Camp California in honor of Browne's home state and the many fellow Commonwealers who had set out from there (and were still a long way off from the East). More than a hundred women in pink and white sunbonnets cheered the famous travelers from a big red bridge that overlooked the canal. A delegation of six young girls formally greeted Coxey and Browne at ground level; Browne awarded them all honorary membership badges. Some number of the Coxeyites, perhaps as many as twenty, parted company with the Commonweal at this point to seek work as fisherman and mule whackers along the canal. A handful remained in those jobs a decade later.[51]

While they were all camped at Williamsport, Browne caught the bugler, "Tooting" Charley, in a state of inebriation and ordered him gone. The bugler grasped Browne in a big bear hug and begged for a second chance, but Browne held firm, and the bugler sadly departed. Coxey, meanwhile, had some other difficulties. After losing his balance and tumbling into the canal, he needed a clean shirt to change into. His supply had decreased when the astrologer "Cyclone" Kirkland allegedly made off with a few, and now his last clean shirt was missing. He suspected at first that Bozarro had it, but then he learned that Jesse had "borrowed" it the night before to call on a girl in Hancock, where they had stopped. Coxey soon received some even more dismaying news: Bozarro had just passed through, claiming to be the Commonweal's advance guard, and had collected $30 under that pretense. To keep Bozarro from making any such claim in Washington, Coxey sent a delegation there: two men named Smith, both Civil War veterans, one Union and one Confederate.[52] (Like the naming of one of their earlier camps for General Grant and one for General Lee, this gesture fit in with the pervasive trend toward commemorating Civil War glories in ways that North and South could share—often at the expense of any northern white commitment to civil rights.)[53]

The Commonweal of Christ awoke Friday morning, April 20, at Camp California in Williamsport and marched to their next spot, Hagerstown. That morning, they encountered a toll booth, whose gatekeeper had no intention of exempting them from paying. Browne admonished the man: "This is another instance where the money power has been putting barriers in the way of people trying to make an honest living." When this drew no concession, Christ's Cerebellum then had the American flag brought forth. He now asked the toll collector, "Dare you forbid the stars and stripes to pass?" "The stars and stripes may pass," the collector rejoined, "but the commonweal must pay toll." Coxey and Browne reluctantly paid the requisite ninety-eight cents.[54] They remained at Hagerstown (Camp Yorktown) for three days.

Behind them in the Midwest, more activity spawned by the economic crisis was getting under way. On April 21, 1894, the United Mine Workers of America, led by John McBride, Coxey's friend from Massillon, voted to go on strike. Though most coal miners did not belong to the union, the strike was widespread, especially in the Midwest and in Pennsylvania. Many of the mine owners did not at first even object to the action, as its primary purpose was to create a coal shortage, which would bring in a higher price for the output. Because some mines still operated, especially in Virginia and West Virginia, McBride worked out an agreement with railroad union leader Eugene V. Debs, by which members of the American Railway Union would not work on trains that transported coal from those mines. The strike started out peacefully but grew confrontational in May and then ended in defeat for the workers in June. The Pullman strike was not long behind.[55]

On to Washington

As newspapers kept their readers abreast of every power struggle, baseball game, reincarnation sermon, and bear hug in the day-to-day Coxey chronicles, they also reported on the police and military operations under way in Washington. As early as the day before the march began, the *Washington Post* quoted the sections of the 1882 Act to Regulate the Use of the Capitol Grounds, which Major Moore, chief of the Metropolitan Police, intended to use against Coxey and his associates. Section 5 of the law provided that "it is forbidden to . . . make any harangue or oration, or utter loud, threatening or abusive language," while section 6 declared that "it is forbidden to parade, stand, or move in processions or assemblages, or display any flag, banner, or device designed or adapted to bring into public notice any party, organization, or movement."[56] Special assistant attorney James L. Pugh assured readers that Coxey's wealth would not make him immune to arrest for vagrancy if police needed that charge as well. Throughout April the *Post* reminded its readers of these intentions. On April 15, just pages after the blow-by-blow narrative of the Browne-Bozarro quarrel on the road to Frostburg, the *Post* again printed excerpts from the Capitol Grounds Act, along with a quotation from one legislator to the effect that the original author of that law must have been "endowed with the spirit of prophecy."[57]

On April 23, Washington's three district commissioners issued a formal statement condemning the Coxey movement. Noting that "the constitutional right of petition does not justify methods dangerous to peace and good order, which threaten the quiet of the National Capital," and that "no possible good can come of such a gathering" as the one planned by Coxey, the commissioners declared that "the laws in force in the District of Columbia are adequate for every emergency, and will be strictly enforced." The Metropolitan Police underwent special drills throughout April, and 1,600 district militia troops under the command of General Allan Ordway were on the ready. In case this did not suffice, the federal government had all soldiers and marines based anywhere near the capital district on full alert.[58]

In the halls of Congress, spirited debates took place. Significantly, Congress most decisively did *not* expend time discussing whether to launch a program issuing paper currency and employing the unemployed to build good roads. Senator Peffer made plain when he introduced Coxey's bills that he did so merely as a courtesy, not out of agreement with their contents. Even so, as Congress debated what sort of reception it should render to the Commonweal and the related question of what constituted a legitimate means of petitioning the government for a redress of grievances, it was mainly the lawmakers of Populist leanings who showed the greater solicitude to the Coxeyites. On April 14 Peffer introduced a resolution calling for the appointment of a nine-person committee of senators to meet with delegations of any groups of petitioners who might visit the capital seeking an audience. In an April 19 speech Peffer declared that he wanted the people to know "that the Senate of the United States is not that exclusive body it is charged with being, that it is not so far out of touch with the people as a great many people believe it to be."[59]

Peffer's Populist colleague from Nebraska, William V. Allen, took the Senate floor shortly thereafter. He expressed great dismay over the buildup of military and police forces and the intention to use the Capitol Grounds Act against the Coxeyites. "Is that American?" he asked his auditors. "Is it right to deny to such men the privilege not only of entering the District of Columbia and the city of Washington, but to enter these galleries, if they see fit to enter them?"

Senator Allen then referred to the many corporate lobbyists who gained access to the Capitol on a daily basis. "Sir, many of them are met almost with hats off; they are met almost with outstretched arms and words of welcome, and yet they are doing the country more damage and more injury than all the Coxey armies, than all the forces that can be mobilized in this country by men like Mr. Coxey." Allen also expressed sympathy for those Americans who had found that merely sending written petitions to Congress through the normal, quiet channels got them little or no attention. Thus, he opined, the right of petition must of necessity include the right to bring petitions in the manner in which the Coxeyites now did. "Are American citizens coming here for a lawful purpose to be met at the confines of the capital of their nation by a hired soldiery, by a police force, and kept out of the city and beaten into submission if they persist in coming?"[60]

Republican Senator Joseph R. Hawley of Connecticut rose to counter him. "Now sir," he proclaimed, "it is a matter of common sense . . . that the behavior of multitudes around this Capitol and these squares here should be carefully regulated by law and rules. . . . And if there be any patriotism in the misguided company of men near here, or the others who are coming, there are men in this Senate who could address them and satisfy them, I am sure, if they are Americans and have any respect for their country." Hawley concluded by observing that the gentleman from Nebraska's speech "would have been received with tumultuous applause in a meeting of anarchists," having as it did "the bacteria and bacilli of anarchy."[61]

Elsewhere in the city, Coxey's partisans were warming up the crowd. Coxey's official representative in the city, a patent and reform lawyer known as Colonel A. E. Redstone, ran a headquarters for the movement in Rechabite Hall, where Annie L. Diggs addressed audiences in evening rallies. "The movement for legislation as inaugurated by Mr. Coxey and his little band of patriots," she told listeners on the night of April 21, "is not a movement for class legislation. It is a movement for the betterment of the interests of the people. There is not a legitimate interest in this country but what would be better off if Mr. Coxey's plans were adopted."[62]

During the Commonweal's three days camped at Hagerstown, some of the press speculated that Coxey and Browne anticipated a confrontation with Bozarro up ahead and wanted to disappoint him by not appearing just yet. The men spent the first night unprotected from pouring rain, as the big tent had been ripped. Though Coxey and Browne had adamantly refused to see their men aid the profits of a dime museum earlier on the march, by this point they had come to see the virtues of charging admission ("Ten cents for gents; ladies free!")[63] to their own camp to build up the Commonweal's treasury. To replace the ripped covering, Browne purchased a large canvass tent that said "He is Alive!" in big black letters; some speculated that the pronoun had originally referred, not to Christ, but to some unfortunate soul on display in a circus freak show. Coxey left them yet again for a trip to New York, both to oversee the sale of some more prize horses and to procure a few sturdy ones for the home stretch of the march. He did not meet with any notorious anarchists during this trip, according to a report by the Secret Service agents who followed him.[64]

Pouring rain did not stop Browne from delivering his usual oratory to the crowd at Hagerstown on Saturday night. Throughout the day he made good use of the press's condescending curiosity about his quirky spiritual beliefs, letting them know that he would be preaching that week about the passage of Revelation 13 that introduced the notorious number 666. When reporters pressed him as to what the passage meant, he replied, "You need not ask me, for I will not answer. The world is no more prepared to comprehend that verse than a child who does not know the multiplication table is prepared to study algebra. But, the meaning of that verse will reveal itself inside of 60 days." That Sunday morning at eleven o'clock, he held his service, standing beside the composite portrait of Christ and himself, reciting a poem called "Mystery of the Whence" and pointing to pictures of spider-like creatures to explain his reincarnation theory. The Commonwealers, growing hungry while Browne held forth, could smell the food cooking nearby but knew not to show any signs of impatience if they wanted to remain in the ranks long enough to partake of it.[65]

The marchers set out from Hagerstown along the Maryland stretch of the old National Pike, sleeping the night of April 23 at Boonesborough (Camp Daniel Boone); April 24 and 25 at Frederick (Camp Andrew Jackson the first night, Camp Lafayette the second); April 26 at Hyattstown (Camp Henrietta, for the current, ever-loving Mrs. Coxey); April 27 at Gaithersburg (Camp Alice Maria, named for Browne's departed wife), and arriving April 28 at Rockville (Camp Legal Tender, named for the Coxeys' infant son). Visiting hours under the tent, lectures from Browne (and Coxey, when he was there), and friendly baseball games with local teams characterized the typical stopover. Another contingent of wheelmen met them along the way, and one persuaded Oklahoma Sam to try out his bicycle. In the fifteen-minute spectacle that followed, Oklahoma Sam, second to none in horsemanship, showed onlookers that he had no clue as to how to ride this two-wheeled contraption. His reputation suffered no tarnish, though. When along this trek he learned that a stagecoach theft had occurred nearby, Oklahoma Sam took up chase, lassoed the lead horse of the stolen coach, and promptly had the conveyance back in its owner's possession. Also on that stretch, he and several others tried unsuccessfully to help a frantic father recover an abducted infant.[66]

While approaching Boonesborough on Monday afternoon the Commonweal met up with Coxey's Washington agent, Colonel Redstone. Redstone had mail to distribute to the men, and he brought tidings from laborite and Populist allies in the capital. He also reported—with far-inflated numbers—that the contingents from Los Angeles, San Francisco, Philadelphia, and Massachusetts would be arriving in time for the May Day rendezvous. He had nothing but optimism about Coxey and Browne's prospects of speaking from the Capitol steps unhindered, noting both the First Amendment and the laziness of congressmen to put up any opposition. He would not, however, grant reporters' request for a comment on the reincarnation theories of his old friend Browne.[67] Redstone was right about the Philadelphia contingent arriving in time, though even here he exaggerated the force that Christopher Columbus Jones had with him. On the rest, he erred. Kelley's San Franciscans were traipsing across Iowa at the time, Fry's army from Los Angeles was camped at Terre Haute, Indiana, and Stead's army from Boston, having just begun the trek, would not reach Washington until mid-May.

While still at Boonesborough, Browne learned that apprehensions were running high at Frederick about their impending visit and that, according to rumor, a federal cavalry detachment would be on hand. Browne, never one to underestimate the power of symbolic visual effects, purchased several hundred oaken staves and a supply of white muslin and tacks, making for each man in the Commonweal a four-foot staff of peace with a ten-inch white flag and the Commonweal slogan printed thereon—displayed as symbols of peace, but usable as weapons of defense if need be. As they approached Frederick, they met, not the cavalry, but a sheriff's posse, put together, as the sheriff told Browne, "to allay the fears of the people along the road."[68] The fearful townspeople of Hyattsville also gave them an unfriendly reception, foreshadowing conflicts to come the following month. One man, a staunch Democrat, suspected that the Coxey march was a Republican Party plot to sabotage President Cleveland. He then added, "I don't like to see those Negroes marching side by side with the white men. It don't seem right nor just."[69]

In truth, the people along the road need not have feared the Commonweal. Though it fell short of being an army in any literal sense, discipline still prevailed. Even those who thought the worst of the Coxeyites could concede some points after seeing them up close. "It is a mistake that has been encouraged by many papers," the *Washington Post* had noted the previous week, "to look on Coxey's Army as an aggregation of 'bums,' dead-beats, and professional 'hobos.'"

It is true there are many regular tramps with the army, but the rank and file of the army is made up of workingmen, some of whom have trades, others of whom are simply mechanics' helpers, and still others with no trades at all. As mechanics they are not the best class. It is not the best class of men who first get out of work in hard times. They are not the best class of citizens, either, for they are the bottom class that has not enough natural or inherited ability to take care of itself when met by temporary reverses.[70]

While they were camped at Frederick on April 28, Johns Hopkins University sociologist A. Cleveland Hall paid the camp a visit and published an article a few weeks later. Though he considered Coxey's economic theories and political opinions utterly unsound, Hall still found much that he had not expected to see.

Improvised barbers' chairs had been constructed of rough boards with a tree for a headrest, and the men were taking turns shaving each other. One man was being shaved standing up. Others were washing themselves and their clothes with the aid of horse trough and pump; others were preparing their scanty supper. Any tramp with the least skill in his profession would have fared better alone by begging, than these men united with a definite object.

Moreover, Hall reported, chickens and turkeys belonging to neighboring farmers could strut safely in and out of camp no matter how hungry the Commonwealers might be.[71]

Sunday, April 29, the men departed from Rockville and trudged through the Maryland towns of Kensington, Bethesda, and Chevy Chase. They had now reached their destination in time for the appointed date. Right at the entrance to the District of Columbia was Brightwood Riding Park. Its owner, a critic of the Metropolitan Police who relished the chance to help make their job harder, rented the ten-acre fairlike grounds to Coxey for two days for a dollar. The men arrived there in early afternoon on April 29. Coxey named this rest stop Camp Thaddeus Stevens. That day and the next, spectators running the full gamut of social status came by. This being Sunday, Browne could not neglect to run his reincarnation services. Coxey followed Browne, telling the curious throng, "This revolutionary spirit of '76 is making the money-lenders tremble now. Congress takes two years to vote on anything if left to itself. Twenty-millions of people are hungry and cannot wait two years to eat."[72]

That same day, guards at the Treasury building had a brief moment of excitement and suspense. A raggedy-looking man with a makeshift badge and a regulation bowl and cup strolled up to the door and attempted to enter. Instantly, two guards seized him and relieved him of his paraphernalia. "Just as I thought, Tom," one of the guards said to the other. "He's one of the Coxey bums." After some further wrangling, the supposed intruder finally convinced his captors that he was Operative Matthew F. Griffin, who had departed from the Commonweal on the final stretch and come into the city by train. They now permitted him to report to Secret Service Chief William P. Hazen. To his surprise, Griffin learned in this meeting that the sharp-looking man who advocated bombing the seat of government was a rookie operative who had decided to experiment with agent provocateur tactics. The assignment was a test to see whether this novice had a future with the Secret Service; the answer was clearly no.[73]

Monday, the eve of May Day, was a busy day for Coxey and Browne. Coxey learned that day that his procession would have a Goddess of Peace after all. Coxey's ex-wife, Caroline Ammerman Coxey, had adamantly forbidden their 17-year-old daughter, Mamie, to join her crazed father in Washington, but Jesse Coxey had traveled to Ohio, conversed with his mother while his younger sister packed her suitcase and slipped out the back, and whisked her to Washington on the next eastbound express train. Mamie now appeared before her delighted father ready to ride. Browne showed her around the capital that Sunday, buying the necessary attire, getting some elegant pictures taken at a photographer's gallery, and procuring a white stallion. Back in Ohio, of course, the goddess's mother was furious.[74]

The first Mrs. Coxey was not the only one fuming with anger at Coxey and Browne that Monday. While the leaders of the intended march roamed around Washington posing for pictures and regaling reporters, the men at Brightwood Park were starving, telling reporters that the Great Unknown had always camped with them and that Coxey and Browne were probably living it up downtown in drunken revelry while they waited in agony. Reporters even heard a few men suggest lynching Browne, if and when he got around to showing up. Browne finally appeared at three in the afternoon; to his benefit, he brought a wagon of bread to distribute.

Coxey, meanwhile, was on Capitol Hill. He knew all about the Capitol

Grounds Act and the intentions of the Metropolitan Police to use it on him, but he also knew that the speaker of the House or the president of the Senate (the vice-president of the United States) could suspend the law and grant permission for a visit such as this. While he fully intended to deliver his speech on the Capitol steps with or without such permission, he preferred to do it with. Many were thrilled to see him there, and he signed an estimated two hundred autographs in the process. He did not succeed in getting an audience with the vice-president, Adlai Stevenson; Speaker Charles F. Crisp talked with him just long enough to give him an answer: no.[75]

So now there would definitely be a showdown, as the authorities would not budge and neither would Coxey. At the National Hotel, where he was staying, Coxey signed autographs until eleven, then announced that he needed to retire for the night. As he, his army at Brightwood Park, the police, the gathering crowd, and every newspaper reader in the country knew, a big day awaited them on the morrow.

4 Other Regiments

COXEY AND BROWNE WERE NOT THE ONLY ONES to think of a march to Washington to advocate for the poor and unemployed as a good idea, even a godly one. In mid-March 1894 the *San Francisco Examiner* reported on one Stephen Maybell, self-proclaimed leader of the Heaven at Hand Army, who held rallies announcing his intention to "march straight to Washington" and "seize the government of the United States and reform it." If peaceful methods did not accomplish this, he declared, they would "eject Congress and behead Cleveland." This march did not ensue, and President Cleveland got to keep his head.[1]

But numerous bands did set out for Washington aspiring to join Coxey, some reaching the capital, others not. In Los Angeles, an associate of Browne's named Lewis C. Fry, a railroad mechanic recently fired in connection with a labor dispute, organized several hundred unemployed men who camped in an unused warehouse and paraded down the city streets with a banner that said "On to Washington." They set out, followed soon after by another Los Angeles contingent, under the leadership of a carpenter from Colorado, Arthur Vinette. San Francisco spawned the largest single Coxeyite group: 1,500, organized by George Baker, who, after bringing the men together, let his friend Charles Kelley do the actual leading. To the north of them in Portland, Oregon, an unemployed stonecutter named S. L. Scheffler had 500 men, mostly loggers, but with a smattering of merchants, clerks, and skilled craftsmen, ready for action by the end of April. Even further up in the Pacific Northwest, unemployed men from both Seattle and Tacoma, Washington, gathered with one Frank T. "Jumbo" Cantwell, a 25-year-old saloon bouncer and professional gambler—the quintessential frontier type—in the village of Puyallup. The mining country of Montana produced a Coxey contingent in the form of about 200 idled miners who ventured forth with 35-year-old William Hogan, an unemployed mine teamster. In Chicago, a city Browne knew well, Dr. J. H. Randall, a dentist and Civil War veteran active in labor movements, had 450 men ready to march by the end of April. Morrison I. Swift of Boston, more a radical than a populist, led the New England troops, while down south in Texas, a unit came together under the command of George Primrose to travel north and eastward. And there were others still.

Misadventures abounded. Jacob Coxey, for all his many quirks, at least had some idea as a businessman of how to plan such an event, using advance agents and telegraph communications to arrange hospitality several towns ahead. Most of these other leaders did not. A quick glance at the map reveals another big difference: while Coxey and his men could make the trek from Massillon to Washington mostly on foot (though it is unclear how many of Coxey's men actually walked from start to finish), if the western contingents aspired to reach the District of Columbia anytime near May 1, they would need the help of trains. The route from west to east did not lack for railroads, but the men lacked the money for fares. Much of the drama with these western industrial armies centered on their escapades commandeering trains and on the resulting confrontations with sheriffs, marshals, and judges.

Fry's Army

The constitution of the Fry movement in Los Angeles, drawn up in late February, did not explicitly mention Coxey's Good Roads project, instead sounding a more general call for the government to provide jobs to all unemployed citizens. Fry also demanded a ten-year halt to immigration and a ban on alien ownership of property. At first Fry's crusaders, steadily growing in number, hoped to wait in the city until they could cajole or pressure either the Southern Pacific or the Santa Fe railroad to transport them out of Los Angeles. But after police arrested several of them for vagrancy when they begged on the streets, and as rumors circulated of an imminent police raid on their encampment, Fry's men—500 of them now—departed on foot the morning of Friday, March 16, preceding Coxey by nine days. The journey of Fry's army had begun.[2]

They walked through rain to Monrovia, where they camped the first night, and then to Colton, feeding on what donations they got from locals and helping themselves to oranges from the groves outside of Pomona to keep from going hungry. Beyond Colton lay a long expanse of desert with no oranges to pick. Marching through it was not an option. Nor was staying at Colton: the provisions they received from the San Bernardino County sheriff came on the strict condition that they keep moving. Just one recourse remained: forcing themselves onto a freight train at Colton. This they did. Fortunately for Fry's men, the railway crew only went through the formal motions of objecting, then carried them, first to Yuma, then to Tucson, in Arizona Territory. Some of the men rode on the outside, holding on for dear life while getting blasted with windblown sand; some fell off and had to walk, either forward or back. Most arrived at Tucson and received a warm reception with dinner from the local community. They needed that dinner badly: they had not eaten in thirty-eight hours.

After the meal, rather than camp in Tucson, the Fry contingent boarded another freight train bound for El Paso, Texas. It looked for a while as if Fry's men might find a much less friendly reception there than they had enjoyed in Tucson because false rumors of plunder and arson had preceded them, and the mayor had organized a local volunteer guard while wiring the state's governor pleading for reinforcements. Fry, arriving in advance of the men, briefly found himself in jail for vagrancy. Fortunately, a telegram from the mayor of Tucson quelled the alarmist stories, and a mostly friendly crowd greeted them when they arrived on Friday, March 23. Citizens provided a nourishing meal and some wood for campfires. Even so, city officials in El Paso let their guests know that one night represented the extent of their welcome.

Their next intended stop was San Antonio. Fry traveled ahead to make the usual advance preparations. His army's problems, at this point, were about to begin.

Following the now familiar pattern, the men of Fry's army expected to watch for the next freight train, clamor aboard, and ride it to San Antonio.

However, the management of the Southern Pacific Railroad had decided that enough was enough and that the time had come to teach the tramps a lesson. (The storming of freight trains by men without money had occurred daily for months.) First, two days went by at El Paso with no trains. One finally appeared on the third day, and the unemployed marchers boarded it. The train carried them seventy miles forward. Suddenly, it went out of commission, stranding them in the desert ghost town of Finlay.

The men trudged to the slightly more promising town of Sierra Blanca. A five-day standoff followed, with abject misery for the approximately 500 Fry men and a public war of words between Texas governor James Stephen Hogg and Southern Pacific Railroad executive Julius Kruttschnitt. Hogg condemned the cruel actions of the railroad and demanded that it transport the starving men out of Sierra Blanca. Upon learning that Texas Rangers were assisting the railroad, he sent them angry orders to desist. Readers of the *Washington Post* learned that, on March 28, the men of Fry's army were "so famished that their stomachs would not retain the food."[3] Finally the railroad, admitting no wrongdoing, offered to transport the men back to El Paso. Nervous townspeople at El Paso hastily collected money to send their former guests eastward to San Antonio instead. Presently, the train took them east and north, passing by the capital city of Austin. Fry and several of his lieutenants, mistaking Governor Hogg's intervention for sympathy with their cause, announced intentions to march the army to the governor's mansion to thank him, but one of Hogg's aides met them at the depot to discourage this gesture. Hogg, already taking heat from critics for siding against the railroad (one Texas paper had accused him of declaring "a state of communism in Texas"), wanted Fry's men to repay his kindness by getting out of his state as quickly as possible.[4]

Traveling mostly on foot, Fry's army arrived at Little Rock, Arkansas, on March 31, with the headcount reported at 810, divided into sixteen companies.[5] They reached St. Louis on Tuesday, April 3. Walking across Illinois, their number reportedly dwindled to about 300. At Vandalia, Illinois, the Fry contingent split. Colonel Thomas Galvin, a Populist whose ideology called for government ownership of railroads as well as public works jobs in irrigation, led the breakaway group, which refused to walk without first making their best attempts to commandeer some trains. Galvin and his men managed to get to Cincinnati by that method, but met with militia sent by Governor McKinley while on their way to Columbus. After a tense standoff, the men hopped off the train. But then, generous locals at Mount Sterling and Columbus, Ohio, and at Wheeling, West Virginia, raised funds and negotiated a group rate for them, allowing the Galvin regiment to enjoy the more conventional mode of rail transport to Pittsburgh. They could walk from there, visiting some, though not all, of the same towns that Coxey's legion had seen the previous month. Galvin's troops reached the nation's capital at the end of May. Fry's group endured at least two more splits. Fry arrived in Washington with his remaining loyalists, numbering about 125, the last week of June.

Fry's associate back in Los Angeles, Colonel Arthur Vinette, a French-Canadian carpenter, organized about 200 men to follow Fry. They began their walk on April 2. Scuffles over trains occurred at San Bernardino, Colton, and Beaumont (all still in California), with Vinette arrested more than once and spending more than a week in jail. In these confrontations, the area populations were divided between those who sympathized with the men's plight and collected cash and provisions for them (including members of an area Farmers' Alliance) and those who viewed them as a dangerous mob to be dealt with by force. Vinette arrived in Washington on July 25, but with a much reduced entourage.[6]

Kelley's San Franciscans

Meanwhile, in San Francisco, a band of unemployed men numbering 1,500 at its peak in late March sought transportation east. Colonel George Baker, the 36-year-old thin, bushy-haired, mustached laborer who had organized the force, stepped back and allowed the command to fall to Charles Kelley, a labor organizer originally from New England, who had lived and worked in Chicago, St. Louis, and Texas. Observers thought that Kelley looked more like a divinity student or a YMCA secretary than a militant, but he had a personal magnetism that made him a natural leader.[7]

The first leg of the journey for Kelley's army came courtesy of the mayor of San Francisco, L. R. Ellert, who cheerfully raised the money to transport them, not across the continent, but across the river to Oakland. This predictably infuriated Oakland's mayor, George C. Pardee, who thought his city had enough tramps already. The 600 men who made that ferry crossing on Tuesday, April 3, slept in the large Mills Tabernacle building. Many of them owned only the clothes they wore.

Mayor Pardee, determined to see the Kelleyites gone from Oakland on the third day, arranged for the Southern Pacific to take them to Sacramento in a freight train. The men, following Kelley's lead, at first showed reluctance to ride in boxcars and demanded proper passenger accommodations. A police raid on their camp in the early morning of April 6 persuaded them to settle, though they still demanded the addition of an extra car to the proffered six. Baker traveled with them; Kelley stayed behind, intending to organize more men in the Bay Area and catch up. The men had lunch at Sacramento, then continued to ride by rail through Nevada into Utah Territory, with the number of both men and boxcars growing along the way. They picked up several hundred jobless silver miners from Reno, Nevada. After the train entered Utah Territory, the Coxey movement suffered its first accidental death. With the train briefly stopped at Corinne, Gus Holmquist, an unemployed waiter originally from Sweden, stepped into the path of a passing locomotive after washing his face in a nearby pond.

They reached Ogden, Utah, the famous terminus of the transcontinental railroads, on the afternoon of Sunday, April 8. The train now had twenty-seven cars, some of which normally hauled cattle, and more than a thousand men, some genuinely intending to march through Washington, others merely hoping for better work opportunities in the Midwest. Getting even that far, however, proved tricky at this point. The Southern Pacific had brought them to Ogden, deciding after the Fry experience that transporting these wayfarers brought less grief than fighting them, but the companies whose trains went eastward thought otherwise. A series of standoffs ensued, with Kelley's men stranded first at Ogden, then at Council Bluffs, Iowa, then farther east, at Des Moines. Newspaper readers followed the events closely, some seeing nefarious railroad barons tormenting helpless unemployed workers, others seeing the forces of law and order keeping dangerous anarchists at bay.

A rather idiosyncratic alignment of sympathies existed in Ogden, where the Kelleyites camped for five days in the Southern Pacific railway yard. Though Utah Territory as a whole had a Mormon majority (indeed, the religion question was affecting the territory's bumpy road toward statehood), Ogden, by virtue of its position as a major transportation hub, had a character of its own, with railroad workers and their families making up much of its citizenry.[8] The "industrial army" conflict that played itself out there pitted the Kelleyites; the Southern Pacific, which had just willingly transported them there; Ogden's popularly elected mayor, Charles H. Brough; and most of the local populace, on the one side, against Utah territorial governor, Caleb West, a Cleveland appointee; and federal authorities, including the court, on the other.

Governor West first tried to prevent the men from arriving at all. Then, with the help of a court injunction, he tried to coerce Southern Pacific into taking them back to California. In response to West's demands, Southern Pacific's president, Collis P. Huntington, cabled him, "It was in a kindly spirit that we took them, and we believe now, after careful consideration of the subject, that your people will do what they can to help them on to their destination."[9] For good measure, Huntington donated $100. While this went on, the Kelleyites remained confined by militia to the boxcars—which meant that the governor had effectively impounded the Southern Pacific train and militarized the surrounding yard. Thousands of spectators watched, many standing on top of parked train cars for a balcony view. The company tried to force the territorial government to cease using its yards and freight cars as a prison by charging the government three dollars per man per day for the use of the space. The railway company in this instance thus stood with a group of western Coxeyites against uniformed officials—very much an anomaly that season.

The situation escalated when the Federal District Court granted Governor West permission to use force to eject the Kelleyites from Utah Territory. Had he done so, he would have herded them back westward, not forward to Washington. At this point the citizenry of Ogden rallied on the site of Kelley's contingent, and the animosity between Governor West and Mayor Brough surfaced for all to see. Then, before West could force the men onto a westbound train, the mayor decided that "this damned monkey business" had gone on long enough. He took matters into his own hands and went to the encampment. "Boys," Brough announced, "you have said that you were going to Washington if you had to walk. Now, we are going to take you at your word. Get your men in line and follow me." When asked whether militia would be involved, he replied, "Never mind the militia. You follow me."[10] Dispensing provisions that local supporters had collected for Kelley's men, Brough escorted them toward the Wyoming line.

But while they were still in Utah Territory, Mayor Brough allowed them to stop and rest at Uintab. Here, a Union Pacific freight train with twenty-seven empty boxcars pulled in and parked on the side track to allow a passenger train to pass. Assistant superintendent Garret O'Neil was on board. An obviously choreographed performance followed. After the Kelleyites had predictably boarded the train, the conductor passed through the cars and went through the motions of demanding fares and ordering the men off the train for not paying them. Then, after he sent a wire to the Omaha office saying that the train had been captured, the train sped forward. The riders expected to stop at several key points—Denver, Colorado; Cheyenne, Wyoming; Omaha, Nebraska—but the train only stopped at Cheyenne long enough to receive provisions from the cheering crowd. Colorado's Populist governor, Davis Waite, though he had promised to welcome them, probably felt some relief when they bypassed his state. Union Pacific's management had evidently decided to pass the hot potato by shuttling the Kelleyites swiftly to its easternmost point, Council Bluffs, Iowa, across the river from Omaha—long a passage point for the major westward migrations and now a major railway hub.

The Kelley men arrived at Council Bluffs on Sunday morning, April 15, in a train of twenty-six boxcars adorned with American flags and a banner that said "Government Employment for the Unemployed." On that first afternoon Kelley addressed the throng, explaining his western adaptation of Coxey's plan, which emphasized land irrigation projects. "This is the richest country in the world," he proclaimed, "and there is no reason why a single individual should beg for bread."[11] He also assured his audience that the men had no intention of committing any plunder. Here, however, his men had to reckon with a serious game change. Southern Pacific and Union Pacific had accommodated them, but now, all four railroad lines that might take them any further east had just the opposite intention—they would spare no expense to make sure that the Kelleyites did not get any free or even discounted rides in their boxcars. In the process, a new archvillain entered the drama: Nat M. Hubbard, attorney for the Chicago and North-Western line. After trying to persuade Iowa's governor, Frank D. Jackson, to block the Kelleyites' entry into the state, he announced that he would rather shut the line down completely for ten days than allow any free rides on it. Rumor had him also saying that he would rather see the men starve to death or be gunned down than get a free train ride. Governor Jackson, for his part, simply wanted no trouble. The Kelleyites remained in the area for a whole week, receiving more than one miserable saturation from the sky.[12]

Kelley's contingent, the largest of any single group of Coxeyites, also appears to have had the tightest lines of organization and command. Each member had a serial number and a formal identification card. Kelley, unlike Coxey,

embraced the title of general, and he had two divisions and fourteen companies with the full hierarchy of military ranks. Baker, originally the organizer,
bore the rank of colonel. A camp hospital tended to the sick. In contrast to
Carl Browne, with his idiosyncratic spiritual beliefs merging Christianity
with reincarnation and currency theory, the Kelleyites' chaplain conducted
services of standard Protestant theology with a Methodist hymnal.

The men spent several days at a Chautauqua campsite. Governor Jackson
at first had militia watching the camp, but then he withdrew them. Early
Thursday morning, April 19, a detachment from Reno, Nevada, which had
just traveled by train through Wyoming to Omaha, caught up with them, having marched all night in heavy rain to the Chautauqua grounds. Two of the
men, however, took refuge for the night in an unguarded barroom in Omaha;
then one of the two "strolled about the town, watched the new post office
in process of erection," and found an altruistic soul who provided him with
the twenty-five-cent toll for the bridge and a ride to the grounds where his
comrades awaited. The Kelley army now had its newest recruit: the future
novelist Jack London. [13]

London arrived just in time to join the Kelley army for a seven-mile march
east to the village of Weston, where they spent the remainder of the week.
During this time, Governor Jackson was trying to negotiate train transportation, but at this point the railroads would not even let the men ride for *full*
fare. Friday night and Saturday morning, unionists from neighboring Omaha
attempted to help them steal a train—many of Kelley's unemployed marchers
knew how to drive one—but Kelley prudently ordered it returned. Kelley's
judgment also militated against allowing women to join their ranks, but he
made exceptions for Edna Harper and Anna Hooten, two Omaha women who
had helped with the would-be train heist and feared arrest if they returned
home. He made sure that they remained apart from the men while sleeping
and traveling, to prevent any hint of impropriety. They appear to have been
present at the Saturday night campfire, of which Jack London wrote in his diary, "We had a pleasant time . . . singing song after song & it was not till after
eleven that we began to think of sleep."[14] Sunday morning, April 22, resigned
to the fact that there would be no train ride, the Kelleyite Coxeyites began
walking.

During the week-long stretch traveling from Council Bluffs to Des Moines,
a couple of episodes threatened the peace of Kelley's army. Colonel Baker,
who had initially organized the men and then deferred to Kelley's leader-

The Kelleyites were camped for a week at Council Bluffs, Iowa, hoping in vain for a train that would take them onward. From Henry Vincent, *The Story of the Commonweal* (1894; repr., New York: Arno Press, 1969), 137.

ship, appeared that Sunday night at Neola drunk with a woman on his arm, walking in the direction of a hotel. In the court martial held the next day at Avoca, he failed to convince Kelley and the other officers that he had merely been making sure the young lady reached the hotel safely. Kelley exiled Baker, and Baker shook his fist and yelled that Kelley had let too much power go to his head. Somehow they reconciled, with Baker restored to his position by Wednesday. Tensions also developed between the men who had started out from San Francisco and those who had joined the march at Sacramento or later. As the footsore men took turns riding in the limited space of the carriages, those of the latter group alleged that their comrades from San Francisco were receiving preferential treatment. At one point, a Colonel George Speed broke away and took about 200 Sacramento men with him. The disputants healed their rift at Atlantic, halfway along the march, with a prayerful reconciliation at the local opera house in front of an overflowing audience larger than the operas usually drew. As with Coxey's own brigade, those who could not watch the drama live could read about it in the papers.[15]

The Kelleyites walked along a route parallel to railroad tracks. No trains appeared for several days. Then, on Thursday, full service resumed along the line, with Pinkerton guards on board to prevent Kelleyites from trying anything. The trains sent out printed circulars warning against any efforts to seize trains. The Kelleyites did not attempt any such stunt, but a few rocks flew in the direction of the hated hirelings. The Kelleyites also believed that members of this force had infiltrated their ranks as spies. "If any Pinkertons or detectives are caught it will go hard with them," Jack London recorded.[16]

Days before their arrival at Des Moines, the Kelleyites endured abject misery from the weather. On Saturday, April 28, after a night encamped at Stuart, a heavy wind storm blew sand and dust into the men's faces and all over their bodies. Then came a torrential rain, replete with thunder and lightning in full fury. The men straggled into Des Moines Sunday morning, hungry, exhausted, mud-covered, many shoeless and half-naked, feeling certain that no wandering Israelite in the days of Moses had suffered worse plagues. They also realized that they would not be anywhere near the nation's capital to march with Coxey on the appointed day—nor were they any closer than before to a railroad line that would take them anywhere. However, during the next few days, donations of food and clothing materialized, and the Kelleyites and the locals met three times on the baseball diamond.

They spent a week at Des Moines. Barton O. Aylesworth, sociologist and president of nearby Drake University, invited Kelley to the campus as a guest lecturer. The Board of Trustees of this Disciples of Christ–operated campus, viewing the whole Coxey movement as anarchistic, issued a repudiation.[17] Two notables of the producerist scene visited the city for the occasion: James R. Sovereign, Grand Master Workman of the Knights of Labor, and James Weaver, presidential candidate of the People's Party in 1892. Not all Kelleyites appreciated Weaver's presence: some felt he was stealing the spotlight and also discouraging area businessmen from donating provisions to them. Sovereign, meanwhile, apparently wanted to convince himself and others that he was still a powerful labor leader, despite the Knights' having suffered a steady decline in membership since 1886. Sovereign publicly threatened that, unless the transcontinental lines passing through Iowa gave the Kelleyites a ride, there would be a general strike by all members of *both* the Knights *and* the American Railway Union, whose still-obscure leader, Eugene Debs, was about to make his own entrance into the limelight in July with the Pullman Strike. If Sovereign thought he had secured Debs's permission to sign his name to that ultimatum, he was mistaken; no such strike materialized. (Debs did, however, align himself with the Coxey movement in spirit.)[18]

The Kelleyites were in a predicament. No train would take them, and they could not realistically walk from Des Moines to Washington. But then occurred one of the numerous episodes of the Coxey saga that resemble a wildly fanciful work of fiction. The Kelleyites and their community boosters took note that they were along the banks of the Iowa River. So, starting on Sunday, May 6, and continuing over the next several days, Kelley's men, with donations from local residents and expertise from unionized carpenters, set to work building 140 boats measuring at eighteen feet by six feet and one foot deep. Sovereign, who had a shipbuilding background and was still in town, oversaw the effort. May 9, the day after a Washington jury convicted Coxey and his two co-defendants of violating the Capitol Grounds Act, the boats set sail. Kelley's army had become Kelley's navy.[19]

Hogan's Great Train Chase

By the time of the Commonweal's May Day arrival in Washington, newspaper readers had already experienced the climax of Coxey-related wildness, not in any episode starring Coxey or Browne, but in the events along the train tracks of Montana. During the last week of April, a group of about 200 unemployed men led by 35-year-old mine teamster William Hogan—mostly miners, but also several men who knew how to drive a locomotive—seized a train. These men were a subset of the almost 500 unemployed workers, mostly miners of gold, silver, copper, and lead, who for months had slept in whatever public spaces they could find in the city of Butte. Montana's economy concentrated heavily on the mining industry and, in the previous several years, had provided abundant jobs in the bowels of the earth. Depression, however, had not treated this sector kindly. A rough-and-tumble frontier culture, combined with a large, assertive labor union and extensive involvement in that state's Populist movement, had ensured that these men would not feel any shyness about making their demands.[20]

Two factors significantly affected the bizarre Hogan saga. First, the railroad executives by this time had mustered more unity and resolve than before, with regard to keeping the industrial armies off their trains. On this they enjoyed the support of Attorney General Richard Olney and some, though not all, of the federal judges whose courts became involved. Second, both of the operational transcontinental railroads that ran through Montana—Northern Pacific and Union Pacific—had fallen into federal receivership from the depression. (A third, the Great Northern, was paralyzed by a strike.) Under this arrangement, while the familiar executives still sat at their desks and made most managerial decisions, they did so under the supervision of federal courts. Here, a peculiar quirk in the dynamics of federalism came into play. While Congress, with the help of the Supreme Court, had established its exclusive authority to regulate the rates and shipping practices of interstate railroads, the national government had not passed any laws affecting stolen trains. If western Coxeyites commandeered the train of a solvent railroad company, federal troops and marshals had no jurisdiction to do anything about it. When they captured a train of a line in receivership, on the other hand, that circumstance made it possible for a federal court to issue an injunction and then punish violators for contempt of court.

On Tuesday morning, April 24, deputies working for U.S. Marshal William McDermott stationed at the Union Pacific's roundhouse in Butte awoke to discover a few things missing. Hogan's men had already been squatting in Northern Pacific's freight yards and sleeping uninvited in boxcars for weeks while holding drills and public rallies. Olney, from his desk in Washington, had authorized Marshal McDermott to organize a team of deputies, first, to make sure that these squatters did not make off with a train, and at some point to clear them off Northern Pacific property. Federal District Court Judge Hiram Knowles had issued an injunction calling for the men to vacate the premises, but McDermott had somehow not gotten around to delivering it. That Tuesday morning, while the deputies slept, the Hoganites stealthily hitched together a powerful locomotive engine, six empty coal cars for the passengers, and a boxcar for supplies. They had already covered ninety-five miles, reaching Bozeman by the time the bewildered deputies awoke.

The great train chase now began. McDermott's assistant, Deputy Marshal M. J. Hailey, and sixty-five deputies hopped aboard a three-piece Northern Pacific train and took up pursuit, starting at six that morning. Meanwhile, division superintendent J. D. Finn, based at Livingston (twenty-four miles east of Bozeman), directed efforts miles ahead of the "wild train" to obstruct its passage. Finn had previously relayed to his superiors at St. Paul a suggestion from Butte's business community that they just give the men a train and be done with it; he had received a flat no in reply.

After eating at Bozeman and stocking the cars with provisions from sympathetic locals, the Hoganites started the next leg of their journey. They could not go far, however, because a rainstorm the day before had loosed an avalanche, and a huge mound of mud, rocks, and felled trees now lay over the tracks. The railroad company had not caused this, but Superintendent Finn ordered his crew not to clear it just yet. The unemployed miners employed themselves shoveling the massive debris off the track. As they shoveled, more earth caved in, bringing their labors nearly to naught. Finally, giving up on ever having a truly clear track, one of the more experienced engineers used the train's engine itself, equipped as it was with a cowcatcher on the front, to blast through. At Livingston, before a massive cheering crowd, the men changed engines again and added four more boxcars to the train. The Hailey train remained in hot pursuit.

Soon after Livingston, the Hoganites encountered another cave-in, this one set for them by Finn's crew, but small compared to the natural one they had gotten past. The Hoganites cleared the track, then put some boulders back onto the track behind them to slow down Hailey's men. Moving well above normal speed, the train went 340 miles, to Glendive, paralleling Lewis and Clark's 1806 route. Among other efforts, Finn's men had emptied the tanks that steam engines needed to replenish the water supply. This stopped the Hogan train at about 1 a.m. on Monday, April 25. Getting only a tiny supply of water from a nearby creek by bucket brigade, the Hogan train was seriously slowed down. Here, the Hailey train caught up.

Hogan now had to think strategically. He made good use of his awareness that the public was following these events. Coming to a steep embankment immediately followed by a bridge, Hogan ordered his train stopped directly atop the bridge. As predicted, Hailey and the deputies approached, pointed their rifles at the parked train, and threatened to fire if the men did not surrender. A group of Hoganites came out, displayed an American flag accompanied by a Butte Miners' Union banner, and invited the deputies to shoot if they so desired. Most of the deputies were ordinary citizens of Butte whom the marshal had recruited in haste for this purpose, and they realized that they could not kill any of these unemployed miners and then return to Butte with hope of living to tell of it. The deputies put down their guns, turned around, and retired to their train. The Hogan train moved forward, still slowly for lack of a good water supply. The Hailey train followed. Billings lay ahead.

At Billings, yet another cheering crowd and another well-prepared banquet greeted the Hoganites. However, the deputies were not through, and their concern for public opinion had its limits. While the train was stopped and the men were receiving the town's hospitality, two deputies attempted to force Hogan to surrender the train. Confusion broke out, and the unseasoned deputies opened fire on the crowd, killing one Billings man named Charles Hardy and wounding several others. The crowd lunged at the deputies, seizing their guns and hurling every available hard object at them. The local sheriff's men made ten arrests. For those deputies not in the sheriff's custody, an endeavor to stop Hogan's men by now had given way to a desperate struggle to escape with their lives. Those not arrested took refuge in the railway company's roundhouse.

In this region rich in both populism and unionism, the Hoganites had no shortage of community help getting a fresh train suited up for their use. As Finn's men had emptied all the water tanks, local firemen brought out their equipment to pump water into the train's tender. Around one in the afternoon, a cheering crowd saw the Hoganites off for the next stretch of their adventure, now equipped with a hose that could siphon water from creeks. After the multitudes had dispersed, the Hailey corps, diminished in both morale and number, escaped stealthily to their own train, though accidentally leaving one badly beaten member crouched in a sand bin.

The next voice to enter the fray was that of Montana Governor John E. Rickards, a Republican, who wired a request to the president for troops, that they might "take into custody, arrest and hold the Coxeyites."[21] Days away from the arrival of Coxey's own force in Washington, President Cleveland met with Attorney General Olney and General John M. Schofield of the U.S. Army. Olney, who throughout the affair had not wanted the federal government to appear trigger-happy toward the industrial armies, but who also had both ties to the railroads and trepidations about the prospect of the capital teeming with tramps, endorsed the request.[22] The chase ended at Forsyth

Thursday morning. Just as the Hogan men prepared to take possession of a fresh locomotive, the federal infantry arrived, transported courtesy of Northern Pacific. Federal troops arrested more than three hundred, while another hundred or so disappeared into the woods. Hogan, after a few sporting minutes of blending in with the crowd and watching the troops try to figure out what he looked like, surrendered courteously to Colonel J. H. Page. Hogan's men and the federal troops had considerably less animus between them than existed with either deputies or Pinkertons. Breaking up a legion of Coxey's Army was not a job that the men of the regular army relished.

After much deliberation in conference rooms and over telephone and telegraph wires, officials, on orders from Cleveland, transported the entire Hogan army to Montana's capital, Helena, to stand trial in federal court. An exercise in legal acrobatics ensued. Because Northern Pacific lay in receivership, federal jurisdiction applied, but only, at least in theory, if the men could be tried for violating a court injunction. Unexplainably, although the court had issued one, federal officials had not formally served it on Hogan. Even so, the court convicted them of contempt of court and gave jail sentences of varying lengths to Hogan and some of the men, admonishing the rest not to steal any more trains and then sending them away to figure out their next move. Several hundred men, with assistance from the city of Helena, set out on flatboats along the Missouri River. The historical record last finds the Hoganites at St. Louis, Missouri, in July. Only a few of Hogan's more intrepid miners appear to have reached the nation's capital. Hogan, in jail while the river excursion took place, got a job upon his release and made a quiet exit from the Coxey saga.

State lines sometimes made a difference for the handling of train thefts. When Scheffler's men, mostly loggers from Portland, boldly pirated a Union Pacific train on April 28, they received no objections from the state's Populist governor Sylvester Pennoyer and very lenient treatment from Federal District Court Judge Charles B. Bellinger. After reaching eastern Oregon, the men changed their tactic from commandeering a train wholesale to hopping rides on trains in small bands. When the railroad did not fight them off, they breathed easily—until they discovered that the Union Pacific was simply contriving to get them into Idaho, whose Federal District Court had a less Coxey-friendly judge, James H. Beatty. As these episodes became more frequent in May, Populist governors like Pennoyer of Washington, Lewelling of Kansas, and Waite of Colorado drew criticism for their sympathetic attitudes toward the industrial armies. Lewelling called the Coxey movement "an earnest and vigorous protest against the injustice and tyranny of the age."[23]

Chicago, Boston, and Many More

In Chicago, during the week of April 23, a venture to help the Kelleyites turned almost accidentally into the creation of a new Chicago contingent bound for Washington. First, a group of supporters of the Coxey movement heard that Charles Kelley's men might make a stopover in their city. This group quickly formed a committee, set up a headquarters in a donated office, and went to work soliciting provisions. William League, owner of a barrel factory that had been idled by competition from convict labor, made his factory available as lodging for the Kelleyites. Kelley's regiment never did visit Chicago, but in the meantime, a groundswell of interest in joining the movement arose among Chicago's unemployed. One of the committee members, Dr. J. H. Randall, a veteran of both Greenback politics and the Union army in the Civil War, found himself elected commander, and League's barrel factory on Rawson Street became, rather than overnight lodging for Kelley's army, the barracks for Randall's.

As noted, Chicago had considerable unionist and Populist activity as well as militant radicalism, and critics of the prevailing economic order could mingle freely even when their precise theories for remedy differed. Thus, in a major rally just days before their departure, Randall's industrials heard a rousing speech from Lucy Parsons, though not by invitation of Randall, who most decidedly did not share her radical orientation. Henry Vincent, while putting the finishing touches on his official history of the Commonweal of Christ, took part in the organizing, and found some amusement in how clearly he could recognize police spies in the ranks: "They insist that they are out of work and at the same time smoke meerschaum pipes and wear yachting caps. They have a cunning look and are inclined to be attending to the business of every company."[24] About 450 men marched forth from Chicago on May 1, the same day Coxey visited the Capitol and Vincent released his book. After a grueling hike, with much attrition and some schisms, Randall and a nominal fraction of the starting lineup arrived in Washington in mid-July.[25]

Morrison Isaac Swift, who led a brigade from Boston, did not claim to be a Coxey disciple, but his actions showed a clear Coxey influence and inspiration. Swift, who earned a PhD degree in philosophy from Johns Hopkins

University, which he later tried to return, was a prolific author of critical social commentaries both before and after the Coxey march. Calling himself a socialist and often called an anarchist by others, Swift led a number of protests of the unemployed in Boston, including a march to the State House with intimations that if necessary he would clean it out. Then, in April 1894, after several months of these local demonstrations, he decided it was time to march to Washington. "We are in sympathy with Coxey's movement," he announced, "but our petition includes a great deal that Coxey is not looking for at all." To Coxey's plan for Good Roads and death to interest-bearing bonds, he added state-run farms and factories; federal control of railroads, telegraphs, and mines; and a constitutional amendment guaranteeing the right to employment.[26]

The march of Swift's army began April 22. An estimated 25,000 spectators, some friendly and some hostile, gathered to watch their departure; the marchers themselves numbered about sixty. The departure festivities turned into a big melee at Boston Common. As they marched through Massachusetts, Rhode Island, and Connecticut, more crowds turned out by the thousands to see them, and smaller divisions with their own commanders merged with them.[27] In New Haven, the industrials received a warm welcome from both town and gown: the trade unions of the city and some students at Yale. The dean of Yale Law School, however, Francis Wayland, ever adept at excoriating tramps, successfully discouraged many pupils in his division from becoming involved with "the soap-shunning, vermin-haunted rabble which may soon be in this town."[28] Following a few more stops to make their demands known along the way, Swift and his men arrived in Washington two weeks after Coxey. Little fanfare attended them.

Others came still, largely from the West, most never getting near the nation's capital. Some were halted by the increasingly well-coordinated federal authorities, others by the limits of their own leadership and resources. In a few instances, unscrupulous or temptation-prone leaders raised money and then absconded with it, as happened to some men from Denver whom Mary C. Jones, later known as labor leader Mother Jones, tried to assist when they reached Missouri.[29] But such misfires notwithstanding, for much of the spring and summer, the nation's capital was a magnetic field, drawing in its direction bands of unemployed men from many parts of the country, especially the West, who were willing to endure rain and hunger to let their elected representatives know that they expected more from them.

Who were the men who made up these industrial armies? Only frag-mented statistics and anecdotes have survived to provide answers. We know, of course, that Hogan's Coxeyites consisted mostly of Montana miners, while loggers from Oregon dominated the Scheffler contingent. The dispatch to the *Washington Post* on March 28 reporting on Fry's men stranded at Sierra Blanca, Texas, described them as "gentlemanly," adding, "there are ministers, lawyers, merchants, and mechanics among them."[30] Three days later, at Little Rock, the report wired to the *New York Times* found "machinists, carpenters, bricklayers, printers, farm hands, and few, if any, professional tramps."[31] Hall, the Johns Hopkins University sociologist who visited the Coxey camp at Rock-ville, Maryland, on April 28, found the men there to be largely "unskilled, un-educated workmen; men just above the tramp class, who are the first to suffer during times of financial depression and the last to regain employment." Of their physical shape at Rockville, Hall remarked, "very many of them seemed like men whom a recruiting sergeant would be glad to enlist for the regular Army."[32] Agent Griffin recalled in his memoir that some of the older men had actually fought in the Civil War, with both Union and Confederacy repre-sented.[33]

Some observers made even more scientific efforts to draw statistics from Coxey's Army. The week that the Kelleyites spent camped at Des Moines al-lowed time for a survey to be taken, possibly by the students of Drake Uni-versity president Barton O. Aylesworth. Of 763 men, 549 identified them-selves as American-born, with most of the rest coming from western Europe or outposts of the British dominion. A fourth of the foreign-born came from Germany, and only a tiny handful was of non-Western origins. Of the 425 who claimed membership in skilled trades, the largest plurality gave their occupa-tion as mining. Political breakdown came to 240 Populists, 218 Republicans, 196 Democrats, and 92 claiming no party affiliation. The religious question yielded 258 Protestants, 280 Catholics, and 114 who claimed no religion. The men had, on average, been unemployed for six months.[34] In Chicago, Pro-fessor Isaac A. Hourwich, economist and statistician from the University of Chicago, surveyed Randall's men while they prepared for departure. Of 262 surveyed, he found 181 to be skilled mechanics in seventy different trades, and of those, 70 belonged to unions. He also questioned 198 of the Chicago in-dustrials as to their party affiliation and found 88 Democrats, 39 Republicans, and 10 Populists.[35] The editor of *Review of Reviews*, visiting the encampments in Washington sometime in June, noted that most of the 200-odd Galvin men had worked in carpentry and the building trades on the West Coast and that nearly all the men who had arrived with Coxey were single, some widowed, and most in their 20s.[36]

The ranks of Coxey's Army included some indeterminate number of African Americans. As noted, Coxey's own division started out with a black color-bearer and a black driver for his phaeton. Reports also indicate more than one singer of color traveling with the band. While Coxey's men were camped at Frederick, Maryland, journalist Ray Stannard Baker informed his readers that black residents of the area harbored "a warm feeling for the commonweal. They always come out and stand in a row along the white-washed fences and cheer lustily. There are a number of Negroes in the army and they all know that Coxey and Browne make no distinction between them and their white companions. This fact has made all the Negro population friends."[37] The number appears to have been small, but how small is a matter for guesswork. One learns much the same and little more from the observation of Shirley Plumer Austin (male, despite the name), who wrote in his generally unsympathetic account of the march that "there was no color line drawn in the army, the only requirement for membership being American citizenship."[38] Also, at one point in May, while Kelley's contingent was sailing down the Des Moines River on flatboats, the *Burlington Hawk-Eye* disrespectfully observed, "There are several darkies in the army and they fraternize on a footing of equality with their white counterparts."[39] With this reputation, it is no surprise that the Coxeyite cause received greater sympathy and support from African American newspapers around the country than from white-run, non-Populist papers. Also consistent with this is the fear expressed by Major Moore, of the Washington, DC, police force, that the arrival of Coxey's Army might set off a revolt of the city's black population. The point is not that there were many black Coxeyites—there appear to have been few—but rather that the public perceived Coxey's Army as a racially integrated affair at a time when Jim Crow segregation was worsening in the South and prejudice abounded in all other parts of the country.

Why did the Commonwealers march? One member of the Coxey contingent told Ray Stannard Baker's readers that the reasons were "being out of employment, without prospect of any change, and the necessity . . . for workingmen binding themselves together for self-protection, to prevent their being hounded down as vagrants and tramps."[40] Though few others left such records of their thoughts, this would appear to sum up the driving motivation. While evidence does not indicate that any one set of doctrines, rooted in either religious fervor or militant labor activism, bound the men together (Browne's theories of the cosmos clearly did not), one does find a firm sense of identity among the Coxeyites as workers desiring jobs—not just individual jobs for themselves, but jobs on a large scale for the unemployed in general. Amid all the disagreements and rivalries found in both the eastern and western divisions, some sense of common cause clearly prevailed.

One sees this even more clearly upon remembering the labor tensions that coincided with the protest journeys of the unemployed. In mid-May in Cleveland, mine operators and union representatives sat down to negotiate an end to the coal miners' strike. Those operators who had initially supported it now felt that it had served its purpose, raising the price of coal, but the operators could not agree—either among themselves or with the union—on the other issue behind the strike, namely, a fair pay scale for the workers. Now the confrontations began in earnest, with miners, assisted by members of Debs's American Railway Union, stopping trains from carrying coal, leading Ohio Governor McKinley to run over budget dispatching militia. To show that he was not totally heartless, McKinley also tried to donate ten dollars to a relief fund for the strikers in Massillon, a gesture the angry miners refused. The coal strike ended without success in June. The miners could now turn their attention to helping Debs's union in the waging of the Pullman boycott. Both unions, meanwhile, had some other comrades in tribulation to think about: the ones who had just arrived in Washington with their petition in boots.[41]

5 Reception in the Capital

THE CITY INTO WHICH THE COMMONWEAL OF CHRIST marched on the first of May had seen much change since the Civil War, becoming more of a major urban center. The Botanical Gardens, the Smithsonian Institution, and numerous parks with expert landscaping and monuments greeted the thousands of men and women who visited annually. The Capitol building was already a prime tourist attraction. Asphalt paving, a rare luxury in most of the country, made most of Washington's streets smooth for easy transport. Trees, planted according to a precise design, lined the sides of the thoroughfares. Of the four quadrants, the northwest had the largest population, as well as most of the centers of government, commerce, and entertainment. Ornate mansions abounded in the West End. In the southwestern quadrant, business and manufacture dominated. The southeast housed several of the city's African American neighborhoods while still having some sections in development, and the northeast still awaited more development and habitation. Since 1874, a three-man appointed commission had governed the city; there were no important elective offices.[1]

Jacob Coxey hopped out of the phaeton, Carl Browne dismounted from his stallion, and the Cerebrum and Cerebellum of Christ made ready to ascend the steps of the Capitol. Mounted police blocked their way, with one declaring, "You can't pass here with that flag." Coxey and Browne jumped over a stone wall, which brought them right into the midst of the cheering crowd. Police on horseback pursued them. Christopher Columbus Jones, leader of the Philadelphia contingent, also tried to make his way through. Police grabbed him, as well as the plainly recognizable Browne, who gave them a chase and then a struggle. Police held Browne down, pummeled his head, and ripped his clothes as well as the amber bead necklace that he wore as a memento from his beloved deceased wife. Ray Stannard Baker, watching from close by, picked up as many of the beads as he could. Spectators in the crowd tried to challenge the police and the horses. Police panicked and charged the crowd, indiscriminately injuring people with their billy clubs, including, according to some accounts, the African American flag bearer who tried to assist Coxey.

While this was going on, Coxey reached the Capitol steps and began to mount them. Two officers intervened and escorted him back down. As police led him past a row of reporters, he tossed them the written speech he had hoped to deliver. Apparently thinking it imprudent to let the cheering crowd see them arrest Coxey, the police merely escorted him back to his phaeton and ordered him to depart. They did, however, arrest Browne and Jones. Young Jesse Coxie and his sister, Mamie, led the rank and file of the Commonweal, estimated at around 400, to their new camp, one of the unhealthiest spots they had seen since the march began: a fenced-off lot bounded by First, Second, L, and M Streets, once active as a dump for garbage and manure and still smelling of its glory days. A stagnant canal nearby added to the pestilential odor. Spectators of all political persuasions felt pity as they watched the men swelter under the hot midday sun with all manner of winged insects hovering around them. Four of the men took sick and had to go to the hospital that day, and the city health officer voiced fears that serious diseases would breed if the men stayed there. The men did, however, receive generous contributions of food and supplies from merchants and others in the area.[2]

Ray Stannard Baker visited Browne in the district jail that afternoon and returned the amber beads he had recovered. "You're the only friend I've got left in the world," Browne said to him in tears.[3] Christopher Columbus Jones spent Tuesday night in jail. Browne would have also, but two women, dry goods merchant Elizabeth A. Haines and affluent journalist Emily Edson Briggs, posted bond for him. Browne soon declared in one of his military-style orders, "The camp to-day will be known as Camp Briggs-Haines, in honor of that class of citizens who are taxed without representation in legislation contrary to the Constitution of the United States: the women of the land, two of whom bearing the above names of the camp came forward when man was lacking, while Liberty lay manacled."[4]

The Long Hot Summer Begins

In the days that followed the May Day melee at the Capitol, both the House and the Senate held debates over resolutions calling for a congressional investigation into whether the police had used excessive force. It resembled discussions of the previous month, with some of the same voices arguing the same sides. Here again, the lawmakers sympathetic to Coxey distanced themselves from any hint of endorsing his proposals. "Mr. Speaker," Representative Tom L. Johnson, Democrat from Ohio, declared, "that the representatives of this nation should have no better reception for a peaceful body of poor, unemployed men, no matter how erroneous their economic views, than to meet them with the upraised clubs of police, is, in my opinion, a disgrace. It is politically a blunder, and morally a crime; and it can not but stir up feelings of bitterness which a proper course would have allayed." In the adjoining chamber, Senator Allen of Nebraska opined, "the rough hand that was laid upon Mr. Coxey was laid upon the rights of seventy millions of American citizens. It is not the right of Coxey alone, but the right of the American people that I stand and speak for at this time." As a gesture of his sympathy, Allen introduced into the *Congressional Record* on May 10 the speech that Coxey had desired to read May 1 on the Capitol steps.[5]

Opponents of the resolutions also made themselves heard. Many held that, even if the police had acted improperly, the courts could pass judgment and Congress did not need to take up the matter. As in the April debates, the question of how to define the constitutional right of petition received much play. Senator Sherman of Ohio, after expressing profound regret at having to expend precious time on this question, insisted, "Nobody has denied the right of petition. Mr. Coxey knew that any member of the Senate would offer his petition and the petition of the men who are with him, who whatever they might think, whatever hardships they may have suffered, or whatever causes they may complain of, yet have the undoubted right to petition the Congress of the United States." But, he continued, Coxey insisted on presenting his

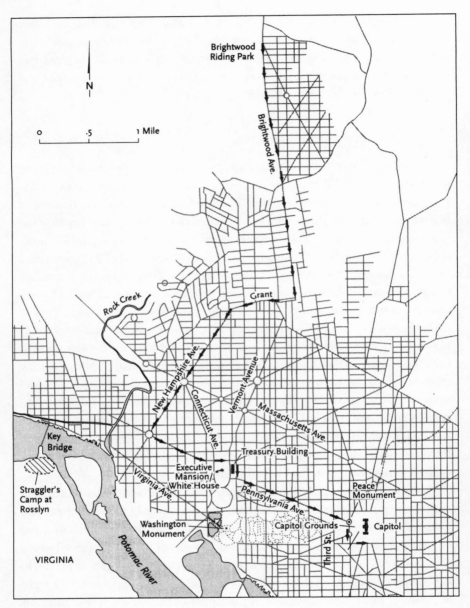

The Washington route. From Lucy Barber, *Marching on Washington: The Forging of an American Political Tradition* (Berkeley: University of California Press, 2002), 31; original from Office of Coast Survey, noaa.gov.

petition on the Capitol steps, knowing this was against the law. Sherman then philosophized about the wisdom of the 1882 law, "framed . . . by one of the ablest men who ever sat in this body." Recalling that the Continental Congress had had to flee from Philadelphia when the British occupied the city in 1777, he suggested that the ingenious design of the current capital city reflected the need to keep the nation's legislative body safe from attack.[6]

Other verbal fallout followed as well. The day before the march and the melee, the police chief, Major Moore, had told reporters, "There is a colored population numbering 85,000 in this city, fully half of whom are unemployed and many of whom are vicious. We could not, of course, afford to permit any demonstration which would arouse them. Hence the thoroughness of our preparations." On Friday, May 4, a group of African American business-men signed a resolution, drafted by realtor Louis H. Douglass, protesting this remark. Among other points, the resolution asserted that "there is no more viciousness among the colored people than among the white people" and that "the perpetrators of outrage and wrong" should "cease to act as if slavery and oppression were still the rule in the district."[7]

Coxey, Browne, and Jones appeared in police court before Judge Thomas F. Miller on May 2, all charged with carrying banners on the Capitol grounds, and Coxey and Browne charged also with trampling the grass. Browne wore his usual costume and smiled for his audience. (On later trial days he sported a more conventional black suit and patent leather shoes, though reporters still noted that his shirt appeared unlaundered.) Jones, having spent Monday night in jail on a hard iron bench, looked decidedly dispirited. Half a dozen Populist Congressmen were present in support of the three accused, with two, Lafayette Pence of Colorado and Thomas Jefferson Hudson of Kansas, augmenting the formal defense team: Coxey's attorney, Andrew Lipscomb, and Samuel Hyman, who represented Browne and Jones.

Among the witnesses, several of the reporters whom Browne had once called argus-eyed demons spoke on the Coxeyites' behalf. One African American Commonwealer named Samuel L. Perry testified, and others cor-roborated, that thousands of police not only stood on the Capitol turf but actually forced members of the crowd onto it, bringing into question whether authorities were really concerned with protecting the grass from being tram-pled. Witnesses also raised doubts as to whether Coxey himself had stepped on any Capitol grass. Another African American man, Edward Johnson, who had received a thirty-day sentence for disorderly conduct, testified that he saw batons flying and that a police officer had clubbed him over the head. Judge Miller refused to hear other witnesses whose testimony would put the spotlight on the conduct of the police.[8]

The jury heard two summations for the prosecution—or three, if one counts Judge Miller's instructions. Assistant District Attorney Alexander Mullowney, noting that Coxey had stayed at only the finest of hotels throughout the course of the march, pointed to the difference in experience and skill levels of Coxey's legal team and the man representing the other two as evidence that Coxey always reserved the best portions of everything for himself. He condemned Coxey as a self-aggrandizing hypocrite. U.S. District Attorney A. A. Birney also delivered a tirade. He called Browne "a fakir, a charlatan and a mounteback who dresses up in ridiculous garments and exhibits himself to the curious multitudes at 10 cents a head." He spewed similar vitriol concerning Coxey, ridiculing the notion that these two could possibly represent working men. Finally, on the morning of May 8, the jury heard from Judge Miller. The law being applied to this case, he said, did not violate any constitutional rights but merely protected the Capitol and its grounds from anarchy and desecration. "The people," Judge Miller said, "have the perfect right to ventilate their views, but they must do it in a proper way, and within the law."[9] The jury convicted the three that Tuesday afternoon. For the next two weeks they were free on bond.

On May 9, the day after their conviction, Coxey had a brief opportunity to present his economic proposals inside the Capitol. He appeared before the House Labor Committee, which was considering a resolution to appoint a joint committee to investigate the causes of the financial crisis and consider possible remedies. Representative Pence, a committee member, escorted Coxey in. Some congressmen came to the room just long enough to get a good, close-up look at this popular celebrity. Browne, arriving slightly late, took a seat beside his friend. Coxey told the lawmakers that for twenty-eight years the national bankers, representing 1 percent of the population, had had the special privilege of issuing money, and that the remaining 99 percent now claimed equal privilege. Representative William Ryan, Democrat from upstate New York, had some questions.

Mr. Ryan—You claim to represent 99 per cent. of the people of this country.
Mr. Coxey—Yes, sir.
Mr. Ryan—On what do you base that claim?

Mr. Coxey—I claim that 99 per cent. of the whole people ask the same privilege that 1 per cent., the national bankers, have had for 28 years. That 1 per cent. have had money at a cost of 1 per cent.

Mr. Ryan—The information I desire is by what warrant of authority you claim to represent 99 per cent. of the people of the country.

Mr. Coxey—I will answer you in this way. You can take the Farmers' Alliance, the Knights of Labor, and other labor organizations, and you will find in their preamble that they want money issued directly without interest. All the orders are demanding that. It is true they have not been voting the way they have been thinking. I will acknowledge that.

Ryan then asked Coxey whether he thought that more than 1 percent of the people were represented in Congress, to which Coxey replied that they were *mis*represented. The lawmaker pressed Coxey further on how he could claim that he represented 99 percent of the people, to which Coxey replied that he was not exactly saying that, but rather, that he was calling upon Congress to grant the same privileges to the 99 percent as the 1 percent currently enjoyed.[10]

That same day, Coxey received formal notification that the city commissioners had declared his current campsite, which Browne had named Camp Tyranny, a health hazard, and that the men must move. At the National Hotel, where he spent much of his time (less pleasant accommodations awaited him shortly), Coxey told the reporters that his men had enormously improved the sanitary conditions of the site and that he did not know where they could relocate. After pleading with the health officer and then the commissioners, he embarked on a search for a new site. The *Post* noted at this point that the army at the camp had dwindled to about one half of its size on arrival, which would make it slightly over 200.[11]

On Friday afternoon, May 11, in the nearby suburb of Hyattsville, Maryland, another protest march took place. The school bell rang, and about 200 citizens gathered in the town square and proceeded to the house of a family named Rodgers. They had just learned that this family, who owned a park between Hyattsville and Bladensburg called Little Spa, had extended an invitation to Coxey's Army to take up residence there. This terrified many in the community. The spokesman for the objectors, a Dr. Wells, asserted that, although the men currently camped in the capital appeared peaceful and law-abiding, the same might not be true of all the others still on their way. He made clear the nature of the fears by pointing out that many of the men in the town were not at home during the day to protect the women and children, adding that some families had expressed the intention of leaving the area for their own safety if Coxeyites camped on their borders. When the head of the Rodgers household refused to accede to their wishes, the petitioners walked away indignantly, some murmuring that they would take the law into their own hands if necessary.[12]

Events in that town the following night almost led to another court-room battle over free speech and assembly. As locals met in the Hyattsville town hall to prepare a proper nonwelcome for the expected visitors, Coxey, Browne, and a few followers (not the actual army) showed up with the panorama wagon in apparent hopes of drumming up support for their cause. A delegation emerged from the hall and told Coxey that he could not speak in their town. A deputy sheriff of Prince Georges County soon joined the exchange and threatened to make arrests. Authorities did arrest one unnamed follower who insisted on delivering a speech, but Coxey and Browne, after briefly asserting their right to speak, chose not to press the point this time. They returned to Washington.[13]

Resigned to the unfriendliness of Hyattsville, Coxey and Browne accepted an invitation from the owner of the George Washington House, a hotel and bar in nearby Bladensburg, Maryland, whose namesake had purportedly once slept and dined there. The Commonwealers, some grumbling in the process, relocated on Monday morning, May 14, to a lot adjoining the facility. The leaders received free lodging in the hotel, though not free board. The bar did a thriving business from persons curious to get a glimpse of America's most famous indigents, and the Post reported that police had arrested thirteen Coxeyites for drunkenness. The townspeople of Hyattsville stayed on the alert, not entirely confident that the danger had passed.[14]

The press, even while editorializing about the folly of the movement and the bad faith of its leaders, continued to entertain readers with detailed updates on life at camp. The Washington Post, for instance, noted that Mrs. Coxey was enjoying repose in the headquarters tent and that several of the men had chivalrously caught a fish for her. Readers also learned that, on the first full day in camp, a man showed up carrying the American flag. When the gatekeeper asked him for the twenty-five-cent admission fee (still a vital source of revenue), he said, "What! Would you stop the American flag?" The gatekeeper told him that the flag had no bearing on the matter, whereupon the

After their arrival, the Coxeyites camped at several different sites. They spent a week in May on a lot by a hotel in Bladensburg, Maryland, just outside Washington. Courtesy of Massillon Museum, Massillon, OH.

visitor, obviously a newspaper reader, reminded the gatekeeper that Browne had had a similar exchange with a toll collector on the road between Williamsport and Hagerstown. The Commonweal moved after a week to a spot in Highlands, still in the same vicinity, which they christened Camp Bastille.[15]

Coxey, Browne, and Jones returned to Judge Miller's court on May 21 for sentencing. Browne told the court that he fully expected to be convicted on a technicality, adding, "Christ was convicted on a technicality." Judge Miller, in his remarks, noted that the law allowed him to impose a $100 fine and to jail the three for sixty days, and he opined that this case afforded him every good reason to impose the maximum penalty. Even so, he fined Coxey and Browne $5 each for walking on the grass and jailed all three for twenty days for carrying banners on Capitol grounds. Browne quickly dispatched a missive to the Commonwealers at the camp, announcing that "President Cleveland, the Czar of the United States from his throne, in a duck boat somewhere, has finally issued orders to Pontius Pilate Miller, who has carried out his edict."

He further noted that he would probably serve an extra ten days in jail by the terms of the sentence, because he had no intention of paying any fine. When the marshal pulled out a pair of handcuffs, Browne said, "Yes, put them on; I want to be treated like a veritable malefactor." A police van known as the Black Maria transported them. Oklahoma Sam rode beside the van on his horse.[16]

The incarceration of these three leaders did not dampen the Commonweal's resolve. On Memorial Day, the Commonweal, commanded by Oklahoma Sam, Jesse Coxey, and the newly arrived Colonel Thomas Galvin of the Fry breakaway, marched to the Peace Monument at E and First Streets NW. When the three leaders were released from jail on June 10, Oklahoma Sam drove them back, and the Commonwealers triumphantly met them at the Maryland state line. Coxey boldly told reporters that day that he planned a particularly big celebration on the Fourth. When asked whether it would take place on the Capitol steps, he replied, "Don't that seem to you the most appropriate place?" A week later, Coxey appeared back in Massillon, where he received a tumultuous hero's welcome.[17]

The Fourth of July demonstration did indeed take place, though not on the Capitol steps. That day Carl Browne revealed yet another of his talents: female impersonating. The Commonweal had obtained a parade permit from the city commissioners, though for a route that decisively did not include the Capitol, and Browne had let the press know that, because he considered liberty to have died, the parade would include a staging of the death of the Goddess of Liberty and a burial in effigy. That morning's *Washington Post* speculated as to whether Mamie Coxey or Annie L. Diggs would appear in that role. In the actual parade, which entered the city around 10 a.m., spectators at first did not recognize the figure with long golden hair, adorned in red, white, and blue, who led the way on "her" stallion. When the procession approached the Peace Monument, the "goddess" gazed at the Capitol dome, which had its own Goddess of Liberty, and delivered an oration; from the voice, the crowd now recognized "her" as Browne. Next, "she" fell "dead" on the ground. Oklahoma Sam and several others lifted the fallen body into a carriage decorated as the Liberty Car, where, behind a closed curtain, the perpetual showman did a speedy costume change and emerged as himself, in his familiar woodsy garb. He delivered some more of his stirring oratory, interrupted when police officers ordered the traveling show to move along. Commonwealers and their enthusiasts then set up camp at a field called Mulligan's Grove for an afternoon of games, music, and still more speeches. That evening Browne preached a funeral sermon for the Goddess of Liberty, which led smoothly into a review of the merits of non-interest-bearing bonds. Coxey, meanwhile, was down in Memphis, honoring a speaking engagement that he had known about even when he announced these festivities.[18]

Indeed, as the summer of '94 wore on, Coxey had less and less time for his army. Already he had begun entertaining hopes of walking up the Capitol steps, not as Christ's Cerebrum, but as one of the lawmakers. Just before his sentencing in Judge Miller's court, his fellow Populists in Ohio nominated him for a seat in Congress. While most of the press and much of the public viewed Coxey as a crank, he held a not inconsiderable place of status and influence in the People's Party, especially in his own state, where the industrial labor force made up much of its support base and where his friend McBride actually did create a Labor Party and merge it with the Populists. General Coxey's own role in working to build this coalition kept him busy.

Eugene V. Debs certainly did not consider Coxey a crank. "It would require the genius of a Milton, or a Dante to describe those Coxey armies," Debs declared in his keynote address at the American Railway Union's (ARU) convention in Chicago on June 12, two days after the Coxey trio's release from jail in Washington. "These wretched men heard the cry, 'On to Washington!' and they responded." They marched for "laws that would rekindle the last remaining spark of hope, that their future would be relieved of some of the horrors of hunger and nakedness." Unfortunately, he continued, authorities cared more about the sacredness of the Capitol grass. "Congress has ears, but it will not listen to the tale of their woes; congress has eyes, but it will not look upon rags and wretchedness; congress has tongues, but they do not move when human woes demand words of sympathy and condolence."

After paying tribute to the Coxeyites and blasting the authorities who had jailed the three heroic leaders, Debs proceeded to address another set of unfortunate workers who had had enough and were fighting back: the striking employees of the Pullman Palace Car Company in Illinois, whose pay the company had cut while keeping their rent as high as ever. Debs colorfully characterized George Pullman as an "intimate friend of his satanic majesty." "So devoutly has Pullman robbed the Pullman employees," Debs declared, "so religiously has he cut down wages, so piously has he made his retainers economize to prolong starvation, so happily are the principles of Pullman blended with the policy of the proprietor of the lake of fire and brimstone, that the biography of the one would do for the history of the other." He called the company actions "a terrible illustration of corporate greed, and heartlessness, and pharisaical fraud which for years has prevailed in this country, and which has created conditions, in the presence of which, the stoutest hearts take alarm."[19] The delegates responded with a vote to support the Pullman strike by refusing to work on trains that had Pullman cars. Combined with the coal strike just ended and the Coxey saga in Washington, this vote ensured that the spring and summer of 1894 would be a high–water mark of laborite anger.

Chicago saw the worst of the confrontation. Railway lines that connected with the city had already formed the General Managers Association (GMA), which now stood posed to take on the ARU. Pullman's company, though not a member, had the GMA for an ally. The number of railroad workers on strike was approaching 50,000, many combining sympathy for the Pullman workers with grievances of their own. Coal miners affiliated with McBride in Ohio's Hocking Valley and elsewhere, back at work after their own strike, helped the ARU by refusing to supply coal to offending lines. (Other unions did not offer support to Debs's effort.) At the beginning of July, the GMA began threatening the strikers with the permanent loss of employment on member lines. Workers and their sympathizers, meanwhile, obstructed trains and vandalized equipment and railway property. The disruption of rail service soon threw the city itself into economic crisis.

On June 30, Attorney General Olney authorized the deputizing of willing individuals to serve as marshals, in the name of protecting the nation's mail. (The ARU was willing to ensure safe passage of the mail as long as no Pullman cars accompanied it, but the GMA refused to cooperate. The railroads, acting contrary to Olney's orders, recruited and paid marshals themselves.) On July 2, a federal court issued an injunction against the Pullman boycott. Now the mob scene climaxed. Federal troops arrived on the Fourth to disperse the crowd of about 2,000. By July 5, the mob was closer to 10,000 in size, and attacks on property intensified, leading to the arrival of more police, marshals, and troops. Ray Stannard Baker, back from the Coxey adventure and covering the story in Chicago, witnessed a similar scene when he was in Hammond, Indiana, on July 8, including the fatal shooting in the chest of a spectator standing beside him when troops fired into the crowd. By mid-July, the defeat of the boycott was clear. Sympathetic trade unions tried to call a general strike for July 11, but that only lasted a day. Debs, for his pains, received a six-month

jail sentence for defying the injunction. Back at the Pullman plant, the original conflict dragged on for another month. Many of the workers, hungry and
hopelessly behind in their rent to the company, moved out.[20]

Such events, while they energized conservatives in their demands for more
"law and order" and their fears of a new Paris Commune, also fueled the
demands of laborites and Populists for strong federal action on behalf of the
laboring classes. At an Industrial Conference held in Springfield, Illinois, in
early July, reform journalist Henry Demarest Lloyd, who also ran for Congress
as a Populist that fall, sold delegates on a compromise version of the socialistic Plank 10 of the Political Programme, which Thomas Morgan had offered
at the past December's AFL convention: the government should control "all
such means of production and distribution, including land, as the people
elect to operate collectively for the use of all." Coxey's ideas were thus part of
a larger chorus, and the march a component of a larger groundswell of misery
and resentment in the nation's struggling work force.[21]

"Well, Boys, I'm Mighty Sorry for You"

From the day that the Commonweal of Christ arrived in Washington the
leaders had promised, and city officials had feared, that other regiments were
on their way by the thousands to strengthen the force. An altogether different
reality unfolded. In the weeks of late May, and then all through June and July,
unemployed marchers arrived by the hundreds and added only to the strain
on the dwindling food supply. This came in tandem with hostilities between
the cadres loyal to different leaders. The day before Memorial Day, about
150 men led by Galvin arrived. A contingent of Coxey men led by Oklahoma
Sam met them at College Station and gave them a hearty welcome, and they
marched to the Peace Monument for Memorial Day as one big happy family.
Within days, however, many Galvinites were chafing under the demands of
Camp Bastille, such as having to wear a badge with Carl Browne's absurd reincarnation artwork, and taking orders from Jesse Coxey, whom they regarded
more as a boy than as a commander. Soon, the Galvinites left Camp Bastille
and went to Camp George Washington, the place the Coxey contingent had
recently vacated. In late June, Fry arrived at the Coxey camp with approximately 125 men. The following morning, Browne met with Fry and told him
that his men did not display enough of the spirit of the Commonweal to be
welcome at their site. The Fry exiles gathered their belongings and joined

their Galvin comrades at Camp George Washington. They soon found that the close proximity to Camp Bastille made this a bad location, as it put the two camps in competition for food donations. On the last day of June the Fry-Galvin contingent crossed state lines and took up residence in a field in Rosslyn, Virginia, just west of the Aqueduct Bridge.[22]

Lest *Washington Post* readers suffer any lull in Coxey-related entertainment, the paper reported in mid-June that, from late April through early May, the time of Coxey's home stretch and arrival, police had been receiving reports of an anarchist plot to blow up the Capitol and some other major government buildings, with none other than "half-breed" Honoré Jaxon as principal conspirator. The articles identified an informant, whose name varied from De Matters to De Mattos, who may or may not have borne any relation to a "Dr." De Mattos, whom subsequent articles identified as a comrade of Jaxon's when the latter purportedly arrived and pitched a teepee at the Rosslyn camp the first week of July, or to an F. S. De Mattos, who appears in August assisting Colonel Jeffries in signing dishonorable discharge cards at the same site.[23] In any case, the bomb-plot story appeared out of the blue and disappeared back into the blue within days, dismissed as a hoax likely orchestrated by Jaxon himself. A Chicago editor in whose service Jaxon had once claimed to work found it laughable that the capital police and press had taken the man seriously at all. "At home in Chicago," the *Times* noted, "Jaxon would reel off while you wait specifications for an uprising which in theory would terminate in the holding of a sun dance in the country building and the lighting of a Métis council fire in the Criminal Court building. It was his practice, when he had his daily plot for revolution well in hand, to seek some yearling reporter and impart the plan in strict confidence."[24] Another Chicago journalist was quoted as saying of Jaxon, "He would rather see his name in the papers than eat."[25]

The month of July saw the situation at both camps degenerate. Coxey and Browne had poured much of the food money into the Fourth of July performance, expecting that enough visitors would pay a quarter for that afternoon's activities at Mulligan's Grove to replenish it. They enjoyed no such luck. Coxey, meanwhile, had already departed for a long stretch of absence during which he hoped to raise money for the Commonweal through speaking engagements. (Among other spots, he visited Chicago to show his support for the Pullman strikers.) Just three days after the Fourth, Browne departed with at least seventy men, by that time about a fourth of the camp census, for an expedition to New York to pay a call on Wall Street—perhaps even to "occupy" it. By the middle of the month, Browne had apparently taken the men no farther than Baltimore, at which time he returned to the camp for a brief visit to reaffirm his big plans. This time Oklahoma Sam left with him. The Highlands camp was now devoid of any of the colorful personalities whose escapades had tantalized the newspaper-reading public, though young Jesse Coxey stayed on for the moment. On July 25, Coxey made one last appearance at Camp Lost Liberty (as they now called it) to tell his men that he had done all he could for them. In a sharp reversal of his stance up until that point, he now advised them to go into the city and beg, even if it meant facing arrest for vagrancy, since it would lead to at least some degree of food and lodging. This time, Jesse left with his father. "Coxey's Army" no longer had a Coxey.[26]

Numbers at the Coxey camp steadily shrank throughout July. The camp in Rosslyn, meanwhile, serving as the magnet for the other arriving contingents, grew dramatically. The census reached 600 in mid-July and exceeded a thousand by month's end. Around July 16, a rift developed between Galvin's and Fry's men, with Galvin's followers accusing Fry of chicanery with the money and demanding an accounting, and Fry banishing the Galvinites from sharing the food of the commissary. By the end of the month, this conflict had become moot, as the camp had neither enough money nor enough food to fight over. For a while the men picked blackberries from the area's abundant supply, both to sell and to eat, but that resource had its limits, as did fishing. Men from both camps resorted in desperation to door-to-door begging, resulting in some arrests.[27]

Indeed, what had started out as a protest movement with messianic overtones had, for the foot soldiers, become a basic struggle for survival. From the outside view, an event that had centered first on a harebrained currency and welfare proposal and then on a First Amendment issue had now turned into an intense and concentrated version of the "tramp problem." By late July, police were receiving more and more reports of Commonwealers showing up at people's doors, not only begging for but demanding food. The steady flow of new arrivals at the Rosslyn camp, with reports of more on their way, raised fears. "How many more of these absurd 'generals' are heading in our direction," the *Washington Post* editors opined, "and what number of tramps they bring along with them we do not know, nor is it important to ascertain. The present situation is quite objectionable enough as it stands. . . . If we permit these worthless drones and foolish dupes to remain here in idleness, and en-

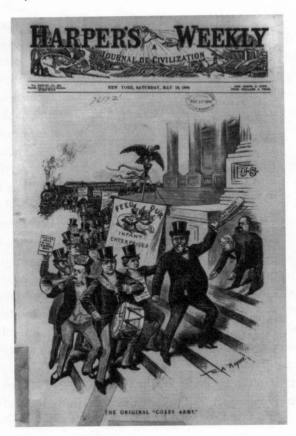

The mainstream press regarded the Coxey movement as a curiosity and a frivolity, not as a serious expression of ideas. Here, Harper's magazine mocks the lobbyists for protective tariffs by calling them "The Original 'Coxey Army.'" LC-USZ62-96769, Library of Congress, Washington, DC.

courage them by alms, it is only a question of time when their numbers will become formidable and their presence incompatible with order and safety."[28]

Concerns in Washington clearly affected the handling of matters out west. In May, while Coxey, Browne, and Jones stood trial and then received their sentence, the train heists continued. Increasingly, the actions of both railway companies and federal judges reflected a consensus shared with Attorney General Olney and others in high places that the Washington-bound exodus of the jobless must be strategically stopped. A series of decisions in the federal district courts reflected this goal.

Beginning on May 28, the two hundred–plus men of Scheffler's army stood trial in Idaho before federal judge James H. Beatty. Because they had hopped rides on a railroad in federal receivership, the Union Pacific, he could hold them in contempt of court. In contrast to earlier proceedings, he applied this charge not just to Scheffler but also to the whole rank and file. Several times in the course of the week-long trial he released handfuls of the defendants for lack of evidence, a move consistent with his ultimate aim of breaking up this large mass into little fragments. On June 5, he pronounced sentence on the 185 who remained. He ordered a camp, as unpleasant in atmosphere as possible, to be built right by the Oregon border—that is, close to where the men had come from rather than where they hoped to go—and had them confined there. Throughout the summer he released the inmates, a few at a time. The Union Pacific, at government expense, gave the men rides back to Portland.[29]

But how to gain federal jurisdiction when the hijacked trains were *not* in receivership? The attorney general had a solution to this puzzle, the same one he used in July against the Pullman strike: arrest the insurgents for obstructing the passage of federal mail—even if, as was the case, the protesters were making sure that the mail trains sailed through undisturbed. Indeed, in some instances it was the railroad companies who obstructed the mail by ripping up tracks to stop the stolen trains from traveling. On May 8, in the midst of a strike against the owners of the state's gold mines, a band of Coxey-inspired miners from Cripple Creek, Colorado, led by John Sherman Sanders, commandeered a train on the solvent Missouri Pacific line and sped across the state line to Kansas. Colorado and Kansas, it should be remembered, both had Coxey-friendly Populist governors, Davis Waite and Lorenzo Lewelling, respectively, so the railroads could not expect much sympathy from them or from the constituencies that had elected them. (In fact, in response to the miners' strike, Waite had made the extraordinary move of calling out the state militia to protect the strikers from a wrathful sheriff and his deputies.)[30] Federal marshals arrested the Sanders Coxeyites on the mail charge on May 10.

The men spent a month at Leavenworth, Kansas, technically prisoners on a military reservation but living the life more of campers—reasonably well fed, able to fish, even fraternizing with the men who guarded them. Authorities permitted Sanders to come and go as he pleased, and he toured the state speaking to Populist audiences. Sanders also met a woman that month; they married not long after. When the men stood trial, the prosecution somehow managed to get a jury that would convict them of obstructing the mails. Judge Thomas of the Federal District Court at Leavenworth dispersed the men among county jails around the state and, like his fellow jurist in Idaho, released them in small groups, effectively transforming a large band of purposeful western Coxeyites into a few tramps here and a few tramps there.[31]

The final dispersal of Coxey's Army from the capital region involved two state governors and the law enforcement agencies and courts under them, as well as federal and district officials and the railroads. At 3 a.m. on August 9, on orders of Maryland's governor Frank Brown, a special police force from Baltimore paid a surprise visit to Coxey's Highlands camp and arrested nearly all of its inhabitants for vagrancy. Police allowed five of the men to remain in the camp for three more days, including one Marshal Bullock; Jesse Coxey, who had apparently returned, reportedly escaped arrest by hiding under a bed. Christopher Columbus Jones and one Marshal McKee were among those taken into custody. Police marched the men to a justice of the peace in Hyattsville, who sentenced them to three months in the House of Correction in Baltimore. The next day's *Washington Post* put the number of incarcerated Coxeyites at 102.[32]

At the Rosslyn camp, authorities that second week of August successfully persuaded large numbers from Kelley's and Galvin's armies to accept transportation back west. Those remaining were now mostly the followers of Fry from Los Angeles and "Jumbo" Cantwell from Seattle. But state authorities still understood many more to be en route. A particularly energetic commander from Seattle, Edward J. Jeffries, showed up with forty men on August 6, promising the arrival of hundreds more while planning the following year's march. For area officials, this heightened the urgency. In the early morning of August 11, as the men at Rosslyn were sitting down to breakfast, they received a surprise visit from a Virginia militia unit led by Adjutant General Charles J. Anderson, who greeted them with the words, "Well, boys, I'm mighty sorry for you, but you must leave this place by order of the governor of Virginia." Some had to carry their breakfast and coffee with them. Several men paraded a flag past Anderson, who took off his hat and saluted it. The troops burned the camp, depriving the men of all possessions they could not carry, including clothes, bedding, cookware, and flour.[33]

These western Commonwealers spent the morning trapped on Aqueduct Bridge. Sympathetic locals, hearing of their plight, came at the noon hour with food. The men were in jurisdictional limbo, sealed off from both the state of Virginia and the nationally controlled District of Columbia, which awaited them on the other side. The recurring dilemma of local officials presented itself once again: forcing Coxeyites out of somewhere also meant forcing them *to* somewhere. Not until the assistant secretary of the navy, William McAdoo, agreed to let them onto the grounds of the Naval Observatory for three days did authorities open the Washington side of the bridge, at 1 p.m. on Saturday, for the men to pass. The following day, the men on the open field received fresh deliveries of food from sympathizers and sermons from local clergy. The heavens that day also provided them much rain; some found shelter in adjacent stables.[34]

Jacob Coxey, hearing that the Commonwealers were in jail, quickly made another trip east. He gave instructions to a law firm in Maryland to file for a writ of habeas corpus to get his men released. He visited the Highlands camp, mainly to retrieve some horses, and then the House of Corrections in Baltimore, where he met with Marshal McKee. But his demeanor now showed a clear shift of interest. At the camp, when Marshal Bullock tried to brief him on the events that had occurred, his lack of patience for listening so infuriated the five men there that the *Post* correspondent observed him fleeing for his safety on one of his fine horses. In the lobby of the National Hotel, Coxey had much to say to reporters—not about the Commonweal, but about his campaign for Congress.[35]

City officials arranged for the last of the western Fry men to leave the capital by train, permitting them to opt for the destination of St. Paul, Minnesota, where they had felt well treated along their way east. At the station, they sang one final rendition of their triumphal song, to the tune of "Bicycle Built for Two."

> Grover, Grover, give us your answer, do!
> Think it all over, before we make trouble for you.
>> Just set the day you'll hear us—
>> The crowd will be there to cheer us.
> And won't we look neat when we take a seat
> On the grass that was raised for you.[36]

About thirty-five easterners remained at the observatory; the commissioners negotiated passage to New York for them. Some twelve additional men had managed to join their ranks by the time the train chugged off. Meanwhile, in Maryland, Governor Brown visited the House of Correction, met with the

Coxeyites in groups of four, and pardoned them on condition that they leave the state. [37]

Oklahoma Sam, having left Browne's New York–bound mission at Atlantic City, made some more appearances in the Washington area, then accepted transportation to Pittsburgh. Browne's own antics received only spotty coverage beyond that point, but his breakaway band apparently stayed camped at Atlantic City from mid-August through the fall. He finally entered New York in October and was arrested for gathering a crowd without a permit and creating an obstruction on Wall Street. Coxey, at this point, was back in Ohio campaigning for Congress. Effectively, the saga of Coxey's Army had ended. [38]

Epilogue
Legacies and Enduring Questions

Coxey's activities after 1894 did not find their way into many history books. It was not for want of trying. The year after the march, Coxey put in a bid for the governorship of Ohio. Over the ensuing decades he ran for numerous public offices, including president in 1936, though that year he stepped aside in favor of William Lemke of the Farmer-Labor ticket. He actually won one election: for mayor of Massillon, serving from 1931 to 1933, in a term dominated by battles with the city council. He switched parties several times, while never really conforming to any party line besides his own.

He continued to make known his views on the monetary system for the rest of his life. In each instance, the basic theory, first formulated in his 1894 New Year's dream, remained intact: the federal government should accept deposits of non-interest-bearing bonds from local governments in exchange for paper fiat money, at a nominal discount rate for expenses, and these local entities should expend the money on job-creating, infrastructure-building projects and repay it over a span of approximately twenty-five years. In each instance he adapted the theory to the circumstances in question. Moreover, although his prescriptions did not directly influence policy and his name never made it into any cannon of great thinkers and theorists, he received a significant, almost startling amount of attention in Washington for the entire first half of the twentieth century. He got personal audiences with two sitting presidents, Theodore Roosevelt in 1912 and Warren G. Harding in 1922, and with President-Elect Franklin D. Roosevelt in Warm Springs, Georgia, at the end of 1932. His meeting with Harding led to exchanges of correspondence with Andrew Mellon's Treasury Department over whether the government should spend money to expand the currency, with Coxey up against Mellon's orthodox determination to keep fiscal policy (governmental spending decisions) and monetary policy (attempts to engineer the amount of money in circulation) separate. Coxey also testified before numerous congressional committees, holding forth on the Federal Reserve Act in 1913 and aid to war-torn Europe in 1946. In that latter hearing, Chairman Alben Barkley of the Senate Committee on Banking and Currency addressed the 92-year-old witness as "General Coxey."[1]

Indeed, the memory of 1894 never got far from either Coxey or those who interacted with him. In 1914, twenty years after the march that had made him famous—and just half a year after Congress had passed the Federal Reserve Act over his objections—Jacob Coxey led another march, along the same route as before. Again the press followed the progress of "Coxey's Army" from town to town, and again there were tensions and dissensions along the way, this time with a near rupture over money for food occurring between New Waterford and East Palestine, Pennsylvania. The ranks were much smaller, however. Though Coxey started out on April 16 with more than a hundred marchers, the census had dwindled to fewer than twenty by the time the procession reached Canton that night. At Pittsburgh, the police arrested them all for vagrancy. New recruits soon brought the number up to thirty-four. Even so, he arrived at the Capitol on May 21 with nine men, joined now by perhaps as many as seven more who came in from Baltimore. This time the district police allowed him use of the Capitol steps to deliver his oratory. Out in California, Charles Kelley attempted to lead 1,200 migrant farm workers on a trek from Oakland to Washington, but state and local authorities employed the National Guard to ensure that most of the men did not get past Sacramento. Coxey considered leading such marches at least two more times after that, but did not. On May 1, 1944, the fiftieth anniversary of the original day, he returned to the Capitol steps and read his original speech to a modest audience—not just for nostalgia, but to draw attention to his ideas for postwar reconstruction.[2]

Sadly, three of Jacob Coxey's sons predeceased him: Legal Tender in 1901 at the age of 7; Jesse, married with a daughter, in 1912 at age 36; and a son named Albert, about whom little is known. Actually, Jesse had two daughters, one of whom he sired in 1894, prior to the march of his father's army. A birth certificate shows him as the father of one Carrie M. Myers, born in Massillon on October 14. Jesse may or may not have known that he was a father-to-be while he was helping his father on the march. The familial circumstances surrounding Jesse grow even more curious from there: within a few years, Jesse was married to a sister of his stepmother Henrietta Coxey (making his father his brother-in-law), and baby Carrie's mother, Nettie, was married to Henrietta's brother. Solely the vital statistics survive; one can only speculate about what conversations and emotions surrounded them.[3]

A year after the first march, daughter Mamie married Carl Browne. Though little information survives on that union, press reports indicate that the bride's father did not approve of the marriage and that it did not last long, though they also appear to have had a son and lived for some time in California. In 1913 Browne attended a Labor Day picnic in Washington, where he talked of the flying machine he was in the process of inventing, and he shared a convivial moment with the two police officers who had arrested him that day in 1894. The following January, he collapsed and died. The funeral in Washington depended entirely on his socialist comrades to arrange; no Coxeys appear to have taken part.[4]

Jacob and Henrietta Coxey had three more children after Legal Tender. As a businessman with many different ventures, Coxey had his successes and failures, going bankrupt in 1905 and regaining his fortune the following decade. He ran the sand quarry in Massillon until 1929. His marches also earned him an honorary membership in a society called Hoboes of America. In his later years Coxey marketed a laxative called Cox-e-lax, to which he attributed his own longevity. He lived to the age of 97.[5]

"Great Unknown" Bozarro committed suicide in Cleveland the year after the first Coxey march. Samuel Pfrimmer, better known as Oklahoma Sam, returned to Oklahoma, then moved to Montana. He ran a shipping business by horse-drawn carriage for a while, and did some ranching and some road building. He died in 1943. Honoré Jaxon continued life as a political activist and drifter. In his later years, he was also a hoarder (the term at the time was *pack rat*), keeping wall-to-wall stacks of books and newspapers. This proclivity got him evicted from a New York apartment. He died homeless at the age of 90 in 1952.[6]

The Coxey march of 1894 represented the producerist idea that, when virtuous Americans were willing to work, their labor should bring them a living, and that, when this expectation was not met, the state and federal governments had a responsibility to redress this injustice. This put the Commonweal in the same tradition as the Knights of Labor, the Farmers' Alliances, and the People's or Populist Party. The Knights and other labor organizations expressed this with their demands for labor laws. The Alliances and the Populist Party did so with their calls for the federal government to provide low-interest loans to farmers and take ownership of railroads and public utilities for the common good. The Coxeyites followed suit in 1894 by calling for the federal government to provide jobs to the unemployed through massive public works projects. That Coxey's vision of the struggle embraced not only the industrial but also the agricultural producers resounded in his words at a laborite-Populist gathering in Columbus, Ohio, in September 1894: "The laborer is thrown out of work because his employer has no money to pay him, and the latter cannot buy the farmer's wheat because he has not money with which to purchase it." Indeed, Coxey took an active role in the Populist Party, and his state had the kind of alliance between labor and Populism that the leaders wished they could build nationwide.[7]

To many, all these demands seemed radical at the time, and even those producerists who carefully avoided the company of Marxists and anarchists frequently found themselves lumped together with them. Indeed, questions of who would be seen in public with whom played a part in explaining why Coxey's larger aspiration—a broad-based political party, built around the labor unions and the Populists, on a platform encompassing the Good Roads plan and many other programs—did not come to fruition. Coxey's loss of the election to Congress in his Ohio district that year, alongside the defeat of his friend Henry Demarest Lloyd in Illinois, clearly showed the difficulty of persuading working-class voters to rally as a bloc behind a third party. Catholic voters, in particular, felt loath to identify with a movement even remotely linked with socialism. Moreover, in each component of a prospective coalition—the People's Party, the AFL, and the Socialist Labor Party (SLP)—the faction that favored coalition had to do battle against the faction that insisted on keeping the group's own mission pure.[8]

Coxey and his midwestern associates continued to stand for coalition. He, McBride, and Lloyd were at the December 1894 convention of the People's Party in St. Louis to fight against efforts by party leaders Herman Taubeneck and James B. Weaver to trim from the party's platform those planks that seemed socialistic and to align it with the American Bimetallic League around the seemingly safer issue of silver coinage. The Lloyd-McBride-Coxey camp prevailed for the moment. (Considered too socialistic to some conservative critics, these leaders and their demands were not nearly socialistic enough to impress SLP president Daniel DeLeon.) That same month, delegates at the AFL convention unseated Gompers and made McBride their president. They did not, however, enact the Political Programme that he favored, explicitly re-pudiating the socialistic Plank 10, and a year later the pure-and-simple trade unionist Gompers had his top seat back. By 1896, the play-it-safe faction had captured control of the Populist Party, making possible that year's Democrat-Populist fusion candidacy of William Jennings Bryan on a silverite platform. After Bryan lost, the People's party fizzled out of existence.[9]

Its demands, however, did not. While the labor unions, farmers' alliances, and middle-class-based reform societies did not succeed in creating a single political party and persuading their desired constituents to unite behind it— an improbable feat to pull off under most circumstances—they did succeed in exerting enough leverage within the two-party system that some of their demands came to fruition over the next two decades. Several elements of the Omaha platform, including the direct election of senators, a graduated income tax, and federal low-interest loans to farmers, became law during the ensuing Progressive Era. So did the right of voters in some states, including Coxey's, to initiate legislation and recall elected officeholders. In Coxey's home state, organized labor—which included many alumni of the state's People's Party— played a large role in lobbying successfully for thirty-four amendments to the Ohio constitution in 1912, including the initiative and referendum.[10] (As recently as 2011, Ohio voters used those provisions to reverse a ban on col-lective bargaining for public employees that the Republican legislature had just passed.) Public ownership of the transportation, communication, and financial systems did not come about, but greater regulation did.

Organized labor, by the dawn of the Progressive Era, was indeed gaining in both leverage and sympathy. In this regard the Pullman strike can be seen as a turning point. Richard Olney, the attorney general who went after Debs and helped defeat the Pullman strike, stood behind his actions, seeing the strike as a public nuisance and a threat to the nation's mails. Even so, the use of the Sherman Act against unions made him uncomfortable (his subordinates had used it here, but he preferred other lines of argument), as did the increasing tendency of all federal judges to regard *all* unions and *all* strikes as a public nuisance. By the end of 1894 he was on record as strongly objecting to the action of some courts that, in their capacity of administering railroads in federal receivership, had fired employees for mere membership in Debs's union. After a special commission that President Cleveland appointed to investigate the Pullman Strike and its handling issued its report, showing among other things that the railway companies had paid and controlled the actions of many of the deputy U.S. marshals in the affair, Olney supported a bill, a version of which eventually passed in 1898, calling for arbitration of railway labor disputes and prohibiting the firing and blacklisting of railroad workers for union membership. Politicians and capitalists after 1894 showed an increased willingness to engage in dialogue with those union leaders who did not carry any taint of radicalism, and a number of union leaders, like Gompers, reciprocated. In 1900, when a previously local reform society in Chicago blossomed into the National Civic Federation, it had industrialist and Republican operative Mark Hanna for a president and Gompers as its founding vice-president. (Debs, in contrast, ran for president that year on the tickets of two different socialist parties, which merged soon thereafter.) Obviously, Gompers and Hanna had different priorities and allegiances, but their ability to serve together illustrated the new lines of dialogue and partial common ground of post-1894 industrial America. Gompers and the AFL also exerted political leverage. Though eschewing third party action and partisan alignments, they lobbied for measures—especially an end to antilabor injunctions—and, after 1906, began systematically campaigning for and against candidates based on labor-related stances.[11]

Responses in Washington were definitely changing at the turn of the century. In 1902, in response to yet another massive anthracite coal strike, President Theodore Roosevelt, by no means a radical or an enemy of large corporations, did what many (including the mine owners) still considered unthinkable: he personally summoned the spokesmen for both management and the striking workers to the White House for arbitration. Three subsequent actions in the administrations of Woodrow Wilson and Franklin D. Roosevelt bespoke a continued shift: the Clayton Antitrust Act of 1913, which limited the federal courts' use of injunctions to shut down strikes; the creation of the War Labor Board in 1917, to adjudicate labor-management disputes when the country entered the Great War; and the Wagner National Labor Relations Act of 1935, which required big business to recognize unions and set up a permanent bureaucracy for arbitration. The strength of organized labor—which could agree much more on desired laws than on desired parties—played a decisive role in bringing these about. To be sure, bloody confrontations and antiunion rulings from federal courts still occurred during these years, but in the big picture, labor unions had still established themselves as a force to be negotiated with, not suppressed and repressed.

Congress before the Coxey march had already started to chip away modestly at laissez-faire doctrine, passing the Interstate Commerce Act of 1887, to regulate the rates and shipping practices of railroads, and the Sherman Antitrust Act of 1890, to bring corporate monopoly under control. After the 1890s, regulation of big business continued to expand in scope and to inspire much heated debate. By the time the United States entered World War I in 1917, the federal government had a Federal Trade Commission, a Food and Drug Administration, a Labor Department, and federal legislation singling out railroad workers for special protections in wages, hours, and safety. The three Progressive Era presidents, Theodore Roosevelt (1901–09), William Howard Taft (1909–13), and Woodrow Wilson (1913–21), achieved these enactments, and Teddy Roosevelt pushed for even more—including national health insurance—in his unsuccessful bid for a third term as the Progressive Party candidate in the 1912 election. Many veterans of populism remained on the scene in the Progressive Era to lobby for such measures. More business regulation and regulatory bureaucracy came in the ensuing decades, especially the 1930s, with Franklin D. Roosevelt and the New Deal.

From Coxey's point of view, his crusade centered, more than on any of these issues, on the money question. Challenging the orthodox view that currency must remain at a stable level of scarcity to have value, Coxey argued that the government, by issuing notes not tied to any quantity of precious metal, should infuse money into the economy, allowing consumers to have more money to spend on goods being produced and counteracting the downward cycle of impersonal market forces. The creation of the Federal Reserve System in 1913, though not to Coxey's liking, represented a big step toward giving currency more fluidity. In the 1930s, presidential advisor and Federal Reserve Board chairman Marriner Eccles put forward similar theories and influenced the passage of several New Deal measures designed to put more money into the pockets of workers. Not long afterward, British economist John Maynard Keynes gave an even deeper theoretical foundation to countercyclical theory—the view that the government should offset recessions and depressions with spending. Minus the emphasis on non-interest-bearing bonds, this idea closely echoed Coxey.

In a move many would have held unthinkable in the nineteenth century, in 1933 FDR temporarily took the United States off the gold standard, and the country formally abandoned it in 1971. Today no country is on the gold standard, though the United States and a number of other countries maintain gold reserves. But for all that has changed, at least one key element of the debate has stayed largely intact from age to age. In the 1890s, politicians and economists tussled over whether the way out of economic crisis was to infuse money into the economy or to encourage private investment with more conservative fiscal policies. Today, they still tussle over essentially that same question.

Alongside debate over regulation of business and management of the money supply came the slow and fitful rise of federal welfare policies. Though the People's Party's subtreasury scheme appeared dead in the mid-1890s, the Wilson administration met the demand of low-interest federal loans to farmers in 1916. Beyond that, federal involvement in social welfare evolved slowly. In 1921 Congress passed the Sheppard-Towner Act, providing federal subsidies to state governments for clinics to care for pregnant women and newborn infants—influenced by years of lobbying by Progressive Era reformers, by the desire of members of Congress to court the newly won women's vote, and by the concern of the War Department over the physical fitness of American youth, after the experience of recruiting soldiers in the Great War.

The 1930s saw the most massive expansion ever of federal welfare policy. FDR and the New Deal Congress provided jobs to millions of unemployed Americans, not only building and repairing roads, as Coxey had advocated, but also constructing buildings, painting murals on post office walls, writing town histories, writing and performing plays, teaching, and myriad other ventures. Federal Social Security pensions for retirees and persons with disabilities, as well as subsidies to states for assistance to households in poverty, came out of the 1930s as lasting legacies of the New Deal. Medicare and Medicaid came into existence in 1965, and in 2010 President Barack Obama signed the still-controversial Affordable Care Act.

Countless other measures have enjoyed debate but not passage. In 1945, Congress deliberated over the Full Employment Act, which would guarantee an extension of the public works component of the New Deal any time the market itself did not have enough jobs to go around. However, only a much scaled-down version, the Employment Act of 1946, passed. This law created a Council of Economic Advisors and committed the government only to monitoring the employment situation and pursuing generalized goals relating to it. Thus, while both Coxey and FDR believed that the government should employ the unemployed, that idea did not take hold for the long haul in the political culture.

While Coxey's Army in 1894 did not succeed in prodding Congress to pass the specific bills they desired in that particular year, they were part of a larger groundswell of angry producers who, in the larger picture spanning multiple decades, put the issues of their own struggles on the table and forced lawmakers and others to take notice and deal with them. And "issues" is ultimately the point. Indeed, the most salient thing one can say about the role of the federal government in matters of business regulation and social welfare, in time of economic depression and otherwise, is that it is unresolved and shows no sign of ever being resolved. Americans differ fundamentally—always have and probably always will—on the definition of the word *rights*. In 1944, the same year that Coxey commemorated the fiftieth anniversary of his march, FDR delivered his "Economic Bill of Rights" speech to Congress. Invoking the adage that "necessitous [that is, needy] men are not free men" (one still found the word *men* commonly used to mean *people*), FDR listed a plethora of rights that he deemed every American should have, including remunerative employment, a home, education, and medical care. But this speech carried no weight beyond being an expression of sentiment. One also continued to hear loud voices dismissing any such ideology as socialism and viewing tax-supported public assistance to persons in need as infringements on liberty.

Marches of the unemployed, calling upon the government to sponsor public works jobs, still occasionally occur. In October 2011, as one episode of the larger Occupy movement, protesters in a number of cities focused attention on bridges that were falling into disrepair. An out-of-work ironworker pointed to Boston's Washington Street Bridge and told reporters, "It's built with buck rivets. We haven't used those since 1935. . . . Like a lot of our infrastructure, it needs to be replaced and it can provide jobs."[12] (The Occupy movement, it should be noted, also utilizes the language of the 99 percent doing battle against the 1 percent, a motif it shares with Coxey.) However, the federal government at present shows little or no prospect of undertaking such a venture, and even the New Deal, FDR's 1944 speech notwithstanding, did not set any precedent for calling employment opportunities a right.

Alongside issues of currency expansion and unemployment relief, the march of Coxey's Army also forced citizens and lawmakers to confront another question: What constitutes legitimate exercise of the constitutional right to petition the government? After Coxey's Army, marching on Washington in large numbers to assert a position remained only an occasional phenomenon in the first half of the twentieth century but has become a frequent occurrence in recent decades. Two events in the New Deal era sealed Washington's place for the long run as a site for mass demonstrations.

In 1932, the year before FDR became president, more than 12,000 veterans of the Great War (what we now call World War I), calling themselves the Bonus Expeditionary Force, set up camp in the capital, some with their families in tow, occupying several vacant federal office buildings in the city and having a larger encampment in the Anacostia Flats section. These "Bonus Marchers" demanded that the federal government pay them a promised bonus for their service in the war, planned for 1945, right away. On July 28, on orders from President Herbert Hoover, troops led by General Douglas MacArthur moved in. Not for the last time in his career, MacArthur exceeded the president's instructions: He not only cleared the Bonus marchers out of the occupied buildings in central Washington, with at least one death and several injuries, but also evacuated and set fire to the camp at Anacostia Flats that evening. While Hoover privately reproved the general for his insubordination, he defended the move publicly, displaying the false belief that the Bonus Army represented, not struggling veterans petitioning for advance pay in time of need, but Communists plotting to overthrow the government. The following year, another contingent of veterans arrived to assert the same wish. The Roosevelt administration provided these visitors with accommodations at a nearby army post and transportation in and out of the capital to present their petition to Congress. Eleanor Roosevelt paid a much publicized visit to the camp, prompting one of the veterans to make the famous observation, "Hoover sent the Army. Roosevelt sent his wife."[13] The early bonus came through in 1936. More importantly for the future, FDR's friendly response affirmed the right of disaffected groups to use unconventional means to petition the government.

In the spring of 1941 African American labor leader A. Philip Randolph made his mark on civil rights history and the future of massive protests in the capital, not with an actual march, but with the threat of one. At that time, the United States stood on the brink of entering World War II and had already declared itself the "arsenal of democracy" in the struggle against Nazi Germany. With FDR acutely aware of the need for American society to look free and united to the world, Randolph's announcement that it was time for thousands of black Americans to engage in a March on Washington for Jobs and Freedom represented a formidable challenge. To stop the march from happening, FDR used his position as chief executive to sign Executive Order 8802, prohibiting discriminating in industries that had the Department of War for a customer, creating the Fair Employment Practices Committee to review complaints. While this act did not make racism disappear in either the defense industries or anywhere else, the event carried a powerful symbolic value: Americans of African descent had seen a black leader force the hand of the president, who had otherwise done little to oppose racism in America, with the threat of a peaceful but massive march through the capital. Randolph was still around as one of the principal organizers of the famous 1963 march, even though most people associate it with Dr. Martin Luther King Jr. and his "I Have a Dream" speech.

But what of the Capitol Grounds Act, under which police could arrest Browne and Jones on May Day of 1894? That law remained on the books until 1968. In January of that year, 87-year-old retired congresswoman Jeannette Rankin, the only member of Congress who had voted against America's entry into both World War I in 1917 and World War II in 1941, led a march of 5,000 woman calling themselves the Jeannette Rankin Brigade from Washington's Union Station to the Capitol to protest the Vietnam War. In this instance no arrests were made, but the chief of the Capitol Police directed the marchers to descend only on the rear of the Capitol rather than the front entrance. The leaders of the march obeyed that order, but sued. In 1972, the Federal District Court of the District of Columbia ruled the Capitol Grounds Act unconstitutional in *Jeannette Rankin Brigade v. Chief of Capitol Police*, deciding that the laws that applied to ordinary visitors to the Capitol sufficed to provide the government with the needed protection and that no extra restrictions on petitioners were required. The Supreme Court affirmed the ruling.[14]

Still, the question of limits to freedom of assembly and petition remain unsettled. The Occupy movements of 2011 and thereafter, together with the resultant police responses, ensure that the debate will rage for some time to come. In addition, the increased determination by law enforcement officials to keep picketers of campaign appearances and other events involving high-profile officials (especially the president) at such a distance as to render them invisible and inaudible to their desired recipients has been the subject of new concern and consternation.[15] Such measures raise the question of whether, and how much, the right to petition the government implies an obligation for that government to listen beyond its comfort and convenience. One can expect more controversies and more court cases surrounding these issues.

For years after the march, Americans used the term *Coxey's Army* to refer to anything frivolous or ill-conceived. However, while Coxey's Army marched, even its most hostile critics usually conceded that the venture showed a powerful sense of purpose and that the marchers themselves showed, with the exception of the train heists, a steadfast respect for the laws and—even then—a willingness to endure extreme discomfort and privation to deliver their petition in boots. And, while Populist politicians in Washington distanced themselves from actually endorsing the Good Roads plan, Coxey's Army stirred up enormous support in regions where the People's Party and organized labor made up sizable parts of the population. For all the scoffers who lumped the Coxeyites together with radicals, one can note that no Marxist or anarchist movement in the United States ever saw the kind of outpouring of popular support that the Coxeyites did as they made their journey.

The march of Coxey's Army fit in with neither laissez-faire conservatism nor anticapitalist radicalism, but rather with nineteenth-century republican producerism. It represented a critique of the direction that the late-nineteenth-century industrial capitalist economy had taken. Central to that critique lay the belief that those who labored, or wished to labor, had a right to earn a living; that, when they could not do so despite their efforts, clearly the monopolistic nonproducers had robbed them; and that, to redress this injustice, the producers should band together and demand whatever particular form of government action they believed would restore that right. One can say therefore that, while in some ways Coxey, with his ideas and methods, stood years ahead of his time, in some other key ways he and his army fit right into it.

ACKNOWLEDGMENTS

Among the many people who have supported this project in various ways, I would like to pay special thanks to Edward O'Donnell and Peter Parides for giving me suggestions and corrections on manuscript drafts. I also owe particular thanks to Bob Brugger, at Johns Hopkins University Press, for his kind patience in making this first book of mine a reality, and to series editors Peter Hoffer and Williamjames Hoffer and the anonymous readers who helped nurture this manuscript. In addition, I received some very helpful leads and suggestions on the research from Michelle Ainsworth, Omar H. Ali, Lucy Barber, Rosemary Feurer, James P. Green, Marc Lichtman, V. Samuel Mitrani, and Roman Santillan. Mandy Altimus Pond, archivist at the Massillon Museum, made valuable resources and insights available to me, as did Jeff Miller, grandson of the baby girl whom Jesse Coxey fathered the year of the march, who maintains the fine website coxeysarmy.org. Lucy Barber and Greta Lindquist at the University of California Press were very thoughtful in granting us permission and assistance for use of the map from Lucy's book. Throughout work on the book, I was also much helped over the phone by a succession of Bob Brugger's gracious assistants—Kara Reiter, Melissa Solarz, and Catherine Goldstead—as well as numerous other staff members whom I don't know by name. Bill Nelson drew us an excellent map, Barbara Lamb smoothed out the rough spots in my prose with a fine copy-editing job, and Laura Ewen in the media office is making sure as many people as possible know this book exists. To all of these people, a big thank you. I am sure I am forgetting people, whose forgiveness I humbly beseech.

One of the basic staples in the working life of a historian is the thrill of discovering an unforeseen connection. When I learned from a *Washington Post* article that the last name of Oklahoma Sam, perhaps the most popular of Coxey's associates at every stage of the march and the encampment, was Pfrimmer, I routinely ran an online word search on the string "Samuel Pfrimmer." This brought me a result that I was not expecting: listings for books written by one Samuel Pfrimmer Hays. In other words, I learned in that instant that the *P* in the familiar name of Samuel P. Hays, distinguished historian whose work I've been consulting and appreciating for years, stands for Pfrimmer. Doubtful that this was sheer coincidence, I made contact with Professor Hays, who very graciously explained that he is descended from Oklahoma Sam's father, and both are named after him. He also sent me details from the genealogical website that he maintains. His book *The Response to Industrialism* has taught many history students about the Gilded Age and Progressive Era since he first published it in 1957; there were indeed many responses to industrialism, and I hope that this book sheds additional light on one.

NOTES

PROLOGUE: May 1, 1894

1. Carlos Schwantes, *Coxey's Army: An American Odyssey* (Lincoln: University of Nebraska Press, 1985), 4–10; Donald L. McMurry, *Coxey's Army: A Study of the Industrial Army Movement of 1894* (1929; repr., New York: AMS Press, 1970), 114–17; and Lucy Barber, *Marching on Washington: The Forging of an American Political Tradition* (Berkeley: University of California Press, 2002), 13–14.

CHAPTER ONE: The Gilding of an Age

1. Embrey Bernard Howson, "Jacob Sechler Coxey: A Biography of a Monetary Reformer, 1854–1951" (PhD diss., Ohio State University, 1973, ohiolink.edu), 15–17.
2. John A. Garraty, *The New Commonwealth, 1877–1890* (New York: Harper & Row, 1968), 81–86.
3. Walter Licht, *Industrializing America: The Nineteenth Century* (Baltimore: Johns Hopkins University Press, 1995), 102–32.
4. David A. Hounshell, *From the American System to Mass Production, 1800–1932: The Development of Manufacturing Technology in the United States* (Baltimore: Johns Hopkins University Press, 1985), especially 21–24, 49–54.
5. Richard White, *"It's Your Misfortune and None of My Own": A History of the American West* (Norman: University of Oklahoma Press, 1991), 163–77.
6. Howson, "Jacob Sechler Coxey," 115–17.
7. Roy Morris Jr., *Sheridan: The Life and Wars of General Phil Sheridan* (New York: Crown Publishers, 1992), 376.
8. On the spirit of reconciliation, see David W. Blight, *Race and Reunion: The Civil War in American Memory* (Cambridge, MA: Harvard University Press, 2001).
9. Philip S. Foner, *History of the Labor Movement in the United States*, 2nd ed. (New York: International Publishers, 1975), 1:424.
10. Todd DePastino, *Citizen Hobo: How a Century of Homelessness Shaped America* (Chicago: University of Chicago Press, 2003), 4; Sidney L. Harring, "Class Conflict and the Suppression of Tramps in Buffalo, 1892–1894," *Law and Society Review* 11, no. 5 (1977): 873–911.
11. Herbert G. Gutman, "The Failure of the Movement by the Unemployment for

Public Works in 1873," *Political Science Quarterly* 80, no. 2 (1965): 263–66; *New York Times*, December 12, 1873, 2.

12. Herbert G. Gutman, "The Tompkins Square 'Riot' in New York City on January 13, 1874: A Re-Examination of Its Causes and Its Aftermath," *Labor History* 6, no. 1 (1965): 50–59.

13. Gutman, "Failure of the Movement," 256–60.

14. For a recent reassessment of the affair, see Timothy Messer-Kruse, *The Trial of the Haymarket Anarchists: Terrorism and Justice in the Gilded Age* (New York: Palgrave Macmillian, 2011).

15. Nell Irvin Painter, *Standing at Armageddon: The United States, 1877–1919* (New York: W. W. Norton, 1987), 18–22; Gutman, "Tompkins Square 'Riot,'" 54–55.

16. Richard E. Welch, *The Presidencies of Grover Cleveland* (Lawrence: University Press of Kansas, 1988), 78.

17. Stanley Buder, *Pullman: An Experiment in Industrial Order and Community Planning, 1880–1930* (New York: Oxford University Press, 1967), 49–144.

18. L. Glen Seretan, *Daniel DeLeon: Odyssey of an American Marxist* (Cambridge, MA: Harvard University Press, 1979), 47–115; Foner, *History of the Labor Movement*, 1:493–96; Richard Schneirov, *Labor and Urban Politics: Class Conflict and the Origins of Modern Liberalism in Chicago, 1864–1897* (Urbana: University of Illinois Press, 1998), 81–85, 173–79; James R. Green, *Death in the Haymarket: A Story of Chicago, the First Labor Movement, and the Bombing That Divided Gilded Age America* (New York: Pantheon Books, 2006) , 57–59, 283–84.

19. Edward Thomas O'Donnell, "Henry George and the 'New Political Forces': Ethnic Nationalism, Labor Radicalism, and Politics in Gilded Age New York City" (PhD diss., Columbia University, 1995), 319–320.

20. Kim Voss, *The Making of American Exceptionalism: The Knights of Labor and Class Formation in the Nineteenth Century* (Ithaca, NY: Cornell University Press, 1993), 72–78.

21. Schneirov, *Labor and Urban Politics*, 146, 238–240; Gerald N. Grob, *Workers and Utopia: A Study of Ideological Conflict in the American Labor Movement, 1865–1900* (Evanston, IL: Northwestern University Press, 1961): 44–47; Craig Phelan, *Grand Master Workman: Terence Powderly and the Knights of Labor* (Westport, CT: Greenwood, 2000), 62–64, 138–144; Foner, *History of the Labor Movement*, 2:77.

22. Painter, *Standing at Armageddon*, 44; Greene, *Pure and Simple Politics*, 31–37.

23. Phelan, *Grand Master Workman*, 28–30; Greene, *Pure and Simple Politics*, 57.

24. Henry George, *Progress and Poverty: An Inquiry into the Cause of Industrial Depressions and of Increase of Want with Increase of Wealth; The Remedy* (1879; New York: Robert Schalkenbach Foundation, 1971), 7.

25. Ibid., 455. See also John L. Thomas, *Alternative America: Henry George, Edward Bellamy, Henry Demarest Lloyd, and the Adversary Tradition* (Cambridge, MA: Belknap Press of Harvard University Press, 1983), 102–131.

26. Edward Bellamy, *Looking Backward, 2000–1887* (1887; New York: Signet, 2009), 6.

27. Ibid., 37–38 and passim.

28. Thomas, *Alternative America*, 174–175.

29. William Graham Sumner, *What Social Classes Owe to Each Other* (1883; Caldwell, ID: Caxton, 1966).

30. *Munn v. Illinois*, 94 U.S. 113 (1877); *Wabash, St. Louis & Pacific Railroad Company v. Illinois*, 118 U.S. 557 (1886).

31. Howson, "Jacob Sechler Coxey," 86–87; Robert H. Walker, *Reform in America: The Continuing Frontier* (Lexington: University Press of Kentucky, 1985), 31–36; Charles M. Destler, *Henry Demarest Lloyd and the Empire of Reform* (Philadelphia: University of Pennsylvania Press, 1963), 51–56. Alexander Campbell and others picked up the theoretical torch from Kellogg. On third parties during that time, see Robert W. Cherny, *American Politics in the Gilded Age* (Wheeling, IL: Harlan Davidson, 1997), 31–46.

32. Gretchen Ritter, *Goldbugs and Greenbacks: The Antimonopoly Tradition and the Politics of Finance in America* (New York: Cambridge University Press, 1997), 66–73, 90–104; *History of American Presidential Elections*, ed. Arthur M. Schlesinger Jr. (Philadelphia: Chelsea House, 2002), 4:1521–1523.

33. *Washington Post*, February 18, 1887, 2.

34. Grob, *Workers and Utopia*, 52–58.

35. Robert C. McMath Jr., *American Populism: A Social History, 1877–1898* (New York: Hill & Wang, 1993), 48–49.

36. William H. Harris, *The Harder We Run: Black Workers since the Civil War* (New York: Oxford University Press, 1982), 33–35; Steven Hahn, *A Nation under Our Feet: Black Political Struggles in the Rural South from Slavery to the Great Migration* (Cambridge, MA: Harvard University Press, 2003), 421–425; Omar H. Ali, *In the Lion's Mouth: Black Populism in the New South, 1886–1900* (Jackson: University Press of Mississippi, 2010), 70–73.

37. McMath, *American Populism*, 84–85.

38. Charles Postel, *The Populist Vision* (New York: Oxford University Press, 2007), 137–156.

39. Ibid., 54–56.

40. John D. Hicks, *The Populist Revolt: A History of the Farmers' Alliance and the People's Party* (Minneapolis: University of Minnesota Press, 1931), 160; Peter H. Argersinger, *Populism and Politics: William Alfred Peffer and the People's Party* (Lexington: University Press of Kentucky, 1974), 105.

41. Cherny, *American Politics in the Gilded Age*, 101–102; McMath, *American Populism*, 153.

CHAPTER TWO: Hard Times: The Crisis of the 1890s

1. *New York Times*, February 25, 1892, 3; Robert C. McMath Jr., *American Populism: A Social History, 1877–1898* (New York: Hill & Wang, 1993), 160.

2. *New York Times*, February 25, 1892, 3; Michael C. Pierce, *Striking with the Ballot:*

Ohio Labor and the Populist Party (DeKalb: Northern Illinois University Press, 2010), 164.

3. McMath, *American Populism*, 166–70.

4. Paul Krause, *The Battle for Homestead, 1880–1892* (Pittsburgh: University of Pittsburgh Press, 1992), 12–43; Nell Irvin Painter, *Standing at Armageddon: The United States, 1877–1919* (New York: W. W. Norton, 1987), 111–14.

5. *History of American Presidential Elections*, ed. Arthur M. Schlesinger Jr. (Philadelphia: Chelsea House, 2002), 4:1734–38; Richard E. Welch, *The Presidencies of Grover Cleveland* (Lawrence: University Press of Kansas, 1988), 108.

6. Painter, *Standing at Armageddon*, 115–16.

7. Harold Underwood Faulkner, *Politics, Reform, and Expansion, 1890–1900* (New York: Harper, 1959), 141; *Washington Post*, March 5, 1894, 4.

8. Faulkner, *Politics, Reform, and Expansion*, 141–42; Douglas W. Steeples and David O. Whitten, *Democracy in Desperation: The Depression of 1893* (Westport, CT: Greenwood Press, 1998), 32–37.

9. H. Wayne Morgan, *William McKinley and His America*, 2nd ed. (Kent, OH: Kent State University Press, 2003), 129–32.

10. Welch, *Presidencies of Grover Cleveland*, 119.

11. Faulkner, *Politics, Reform, and Expansion*, 153.

12. Welch, *Presidencies of Grover Cleveland*, 125–39.

13. Steeples and Whitten, *Democracy in Desperation*, 170–72; Samuel Rezneck, "Unemployment, Unrest, and Relief in the United States, during the Depression of 1893–1897," *Journal of Political Economy* 61, no. 4 (1953): 324–45; Philip S. Foner, *History of the Labor Movement in the United States*, 2nd ed. (New York: International Publishers, 1975), 2:139; Carlos C. Closson Jr., "The Unemployed in American Cities," *Quarterly Review of Economics* 8, no. 2 (1894): 168–217.

14. E.g., see Josephine Shaw Lowell, "Methods of Relief for the Unemployed," *Forum* 16 (1894): 655–62.

15. *New York Sun*, August 21, 1893, article reprinted in *The Samuel Gompers Papers*, vol. 3, ed. Stuart B. Kaufman (Urbana: University of Illinois Press, 1989), 378; William T. Stead, *If Christ Came to Chicago* (Chicago: Laird & Lee, 1894), 387–88, accessed via books.google.com; Rezneck, "Unemployment, Unrest, and Relief," 332–33; *Washington Post*, February 21, 1894, 1.

16. *New York Times*, August 23, 1893, 4; Roswell P. Flower, speech at the State Fair, Syracuse, NY, September 16, 1893, in *Public Papers of Roswell P. Flower, Governor*, vol. 2, *1893* (Albany: Argus, 1894), 351.

17. Steeples and Whitten, *Democracy in Desperation*, 84–88; Rezneck, "Unemployment, Unrest, and Relief," 328.

18. Leah Hannah Feder, *Unemployment Relief in Periods of Depression: A Study of Measures Adopted in Certain American Cities, 1857 through 1922* (New York: Russell Sage Foundation, 1936), 155; Flower, speech at the State Fair, 346.

19. Sidney L. Harring, "Class Conflict and the Suppression of Tramps in Buffalo, 1892–1894," *Law and Society Review* 11, no. 5 (1977): 885–86, 894; Steeples and Whitten, *Democracy in Desperation*, 172; Stead, *If Christ Came to Chicago*, 27–30.

20. Stanley Buder, *Pullman: An Experiment in Industrial Order and Community Planning, 1880–1930* (New York: Oxford University Press, 1967), 152.

21. *New York Times*, March 20, 1894, 3; *New York Times*, May 7, 1894, 2.

22. Jerry Prout, "Coxey's Challenge in the Populist Moment" (PhD diss., George Mason University, 2012), 128.

23. Embrey Bernard Howson, "Jacob Sechler Coxey: A Biography of a Monetary Reformer, 1854–1951" (PhD diss., Ohio State University, 1973, ohiolink.edu), 128–30.

24. Carlos Schwantes, *Coxey's Army: An American Odyssey* (Lincoln: University of Nebraska Press, 1985), 37–39; Errol Wayne Stevens, *Radical L.A.: From Coxey's Army to the Watts Riots, 1894–1965* (Norman: University of Oklahoma Press, 2009), 12–14.

25. Donald L. McMurry, *Coxey's Army: A Study of the Industrial Army Movement of 1894* (1929; repr., New York: AMS Press, 1970), 34–36; Henry Vincent, *The Story of the Commonweal* (1894; repr., New York: Arno Press, 1969), 174–75.

26. Donald B. Smith, *Honoré Jaxon: Prairie Visionary* (Regina, SK: Coteau Books, 2007), 95–96 and passim.

27. Willis J. Abbot, *Carter Henry Harrison: A Memoir* (New York: Dodd Mead, 1894), 230.

28. *Washington Post*, October 29, 1893, 1.

29. Ibid., December 15, 1893, 1; Michael C. Pierce, *Striking with the Ballot: Ohio Labor and the Populist Party* (DeKalb: Northern Illinois University Press, 2010), 159–60.

30. Edward W. Bemis, "The Convention of the American Federation of Labor," *Journal of Political Economy* 2, no. 2 (1894): 298–99.

CHAPTER THREE: Petition in Boots

1. Ray Stannard Baker, *American Chronicle* (New York: Charles Scribner's Sons, 1945), 6.

2. Ibid., 7.

3. Matthew F. Griffin, "Secret Service Memories," part 1 of the Coxey portion, *Flynn's Weekly Detective Fiction*, March 13, 1926, 915–18.

4. Embrey Bernard Howson, "Jacob Sechler Coxey: A Biography of a Monetary Reformer, 1854–1951" (PhD diss., Ohio State University, 1973, ohiolink.edu), 133–36.

5. *New York Times*, January 28, 1894, 9; *Washington Post*, January 28, 1894, 4.

6. Donald L. McMurry, *Coxey's Army: A Study of the Industrial Army Movement of 1894* (1929; repr., New York: AMS Press, 1970), 37–38.

7. C. H. Dennis to Baker, March 10, 1894, Ray Stannard Baker Papers, reel 23, container 23, Library of Congress, Washington, DC.

8. Michael S. Sweeney, "'The Desire for the Sensational': Coxey's Army and the Argus-Eyed Demons of Hell," *Journalism History* 23, no. 3 (1997): 114–15.

9. Baker, *American Chronicle*, 12; Carlos Schwantes, *Coxey's Army: An American Odyssey* (Lincoln: University of Nebraska Press, 1985), 42–44.

10. Baker, *American Chronicle*, 11–15; Schwantes, *Coxey's Army*, 40–42.

11. *Washington Post*, April 25, 1894, 2.

12. Throughout this chapter, the town-by-town narrative is culled from Schwantes,

Coxey's Army, 45–82, 141–48, 166–76; McMurry, *Coxey's Army*, 72–103; Henry Vincent, *The Story of the Commonweal* (1894; repr., New York: Arno Press, 1969), 56–124; Jerry Prout, "Coxey's Challenge in the Populist Moment" (PhD diss., George Mason University, 2012), 260–325, 363–64; and other sources as noted. Names of towns and camps are listed in Prout, "Coxey's Challenge," appendix E, and W. T. Stead, "'Coxeyism': A Character Sketch," *Review of Reviews* 10, no. 1 (1894): 57.

13. Griffin, "Secret Service Memories," 918; *Washington Post*, March 26, 1894, 1.

14. Ray Stannard Baker, "Goddess Is Engaged," *Chicago Record*, dateline March 22, 1894, *Coxey's Army, 1893–1894: Scrapbook with Photographs* (New York Public Library Photography Collection), 1:9.

15. Prout, "Coxey's Challenge," 186–87.

16. Vincent, *Story of the Commonweal*, 57.

17. Ibid., 58–61 (both letters appear in full).

18. McMurry, *Coxey's Army*, 57.

19. Schwantes, *Coxey's Army*, 51–52.

20. *Trenton Times*, March 29, 1894, 2; *New York Herald*, March 29, 1894, 6.

21. *Washington Post*, March 29, 1894, 1; *Cleveland Plain Dealer*, March 25, 1894, 3.

22. *Washington Post*, March 30, 1894, 4.

23. Prout, "Coxey's Challenge," 235.

24. *Washington Post*, March 20, 1894, 4.

25. On the press, see Sweeney, "Desire for the Sensational."

26. Philip S. Foner, *History of the Labor Movement in the United States*, 2nd ed. (New York: International Publishers, 1975), 2:242; Samuel Gompers, *Seventy Years of Life and Labor: An Autobiography* (New York: E. P. Dutton, 1925; repr., New York: Augustus M. Kelley, 1967), 2: 10–12; Prout, "Coxey's Challenge," 189–201; *Washington Bee*, April 28, 1894, 2.

27. Baker, "Chance for a Battle," *Chicago Record*, dateline March 30, 1894, *Coxey's Army: Scrapbook*, 1:19.

28. Arthur Versluis, "Western Esotericism and the Harmony Society," n.d., http://www.esoteric.msu.edu/Versluis.html, accessed March 13, 2014.

29. Schwantes, *Coxey's Army*, 51; Baker, "Entered in Triumph," *Chicago Record*, dateline March 27, 1894, *Coxey's Army: Scrapbook*, 1:14.

30. Howson, "Jacob Sechler Coxey," 146; McMurry, *Coxey's Army*, 75.

31. *Pittsburgh Press*, April 3, 1894, 1.

32. McMurry, *Coxey's Army*, 78–82; *Baltimore Sun*, April 5, 1894, 1.

33. Griffin, "Secret Service Memories," 918.

34. Ibid., 919.

35. McMurry, *Coxey's Army*, 91.

36. *Pittsburgh Press*, April 5, 1894, 1; *Pittsburgh Post*, April 6, 1894, 2.

37. *Washington Post*, April 6, 1894, 4.

38. Baker, "Forced to Pay Toll," *Chicago Record*, dateline April 9, 1894, *Coxey's Army: Scrapbook*, 1:35.

39. Schwantes, *Coxey's Army*, 63.

40. Baker, "March in the Snow," *Chicago Record*, dateline April 11, 1894, *Coxey's Army: Scrapbook*, 1:39.

41. Griffin, "Secret Service Memories," 922–23.

42. Ibid., 920, 926.

43. Schwantes, *Coxey's Army*, 67; Griffin, "Secret Service Memories," 922–25.

44. *Washington Post*, April 15, 1894, 2.

45. Ibid., April 16, 1894, 1; April 17, 1894, 1.

46. Ibid., April 19, 1894, 2.

47. "Capital Detectives Tell How, Disguised as Hoboes, They Watched Coxey's Army," *Washington Post*, September 3, 1922, 22.

48. Baker to his father, April 19, 1894, Baker Papers, LOC, reel 23, container 23.

49. "Coxey Takes Water," *Chicago Record*, dateline April 17, 1893, *Coxey's Army: Scrapbook*, 1:50.

50. *New York Tribune*, April 20, 1894, 3.

51. "Remnant of Coxey's Army," *Washington Post*, October 18, 1903, E–11.

52. *Pittsburgh Press*, April 18, 1894, 1.

53. David W. Blight, *Race and Reunion: The Civil War in American Memory* (Cambridge, MA: Harvard University Press, 2001), 87–97, 164–70.

54. Baker, "Coxey on Historic Ground," *Chicago Record*, dateline April 20, 1894, *Coxey's Army: Scrapbook*, 1:52.

55. Michael C. Pierce, *Striking with the Ballot: Ohio Labor and the Populist Party* (DeKalb: Northern Illinois University Press, 2010), 156–62.

56. *Washington Post*, March 24, 1894, 1.

57. Ibid., April 15, 1894, 7.

58. Ibid., April 24, 1894, 2.

59. *Congressional Record*, April 19, 1894, 3842.

60. Ibid., 3843.

61. Ibid., April 20, 1894, 3844.

62. *Washington Post*, April 22, 1894, 3.

63. Ibid.

64. Schwantes, *Coxey's Army*, 167.

65. *Pittsburgh Post*, April 22, 1894, 7; Baker, "Looks for 300,000 Men," *Chicago Record*, dateline April 22, 1894, *Coxey's Army: Scrapbook*, 54–56.

66. *Washington Post*, April 27, 1894, 1; April 28, 1894, 1; September 3, 1922, 22 ("Capital Detectives" article).

67. Baker, "Getting Near the Capital," *Chicago Record*, dateline April 23, 1894, *Coxey's Army: Scrapbook*, 56.

68. Schwantes, *Coxey's Army*, 146.

69. Baker, "Thirty Miles from Washington," *Chicago Record*, dateline April 26, 1894, *Coxey's Army: Scrapbook*, 62.

70. *Washington Post*, April 19, 1894, 2.

71. A. Cleveland Hall, "An Observer in Coxey's Camp," *The Independent* 46 (May 17, 1894), 3.

72. Schwantes, *Coxey's Army*, 174; *Washington Post*, April 30, 1894, 1.

73. Matthew F. Griffin, "Secret Service Memories," part 2 of Coxey portion, *Flynn's Weekly Detective Fiction*, March 20, 1926, 88–89.

74. Schwantes, *Coxey's Army*, 175.

75. Ibid., 175–76.

CHAPTER FOUR: Other Regiments

1. Carlos Schwantes, *Coxey's Army: An American Odyssey* (Lincoln: University of Nebraska Press, 1985), 83–84.

2. The Fry constitution is printed in Henry Vincent, *The Story of the Commonweal* (1894; repr., New York: Arno Press, 1969), 163–65, and the travels of the Fry army appear in Schwantes, *Coxey's Army*, 86–97; Donald L. McMurry, *Coxey's Army: A Study of the Industrial Army Movement of 1894* (1929; repr., New York: AMS Press, 1970), 127–48; Vincent, *Story of the Commonweal*, 165–73; and Errol Wayne Stevens, *Radical L.A.: From Coxey's Army to the Watts Riots, 1894–1965* (Norman: University of Oklahoma Press, 2009), 10–20.

3. *Washington Post*, March 29, 1894, 1.

4. *Dallas News*, quoted in *Washington Post*, April 1, 1894, 4.

5. *New York Times*, April 1, 1894, 1.

6. Henry Winfred Splitter, "Concerning Vinette's Los Angeles Regiment of Coxey's Army," *Pacific Historical Review* 17, no. 1 (1948): 29–36.

7. The general Kelley narrative appears in Schwantes, *Coxey's Army*, 98–141; McMurry, *Coxey's Army*, 149–96; Vincent, *Story of the Commonweal*, 125–62.

8. Thomas G. Alexander, "Ogden, a Federal Colony in Utah," *Utah Historical Quarterly* 47, no. 3 (1979): 291–309.

9. Schwantes, *Coxey's Army*, 106.

10. Ibid., 109.

11. Ibid., 116.

12. *Idaho Statesman*, April 21, 1894, 1; *Tacoma Daily News*, April 26, 1894, 2.

13. Jack London, "The Tramp Diary," April 19, 1894 entry, in *Jack London on the Road: The Tramp Diary and Other Hobo Writings*, ed. Richard W. Etulain (Logan: Utah State University Press, 1979), 40.

14. Ibid., April 21, 1894 entry, 44.

15. *New York Times*, April 24, 1894, 1; April 26, 1894, 2.

16. London, "Tramp Diary," April 26, 1894 entry, 48.

17. *Washington Post*, May 2, 1894, 2; McMurry, *Coxey's Army*, 187; Lester G. McAllister and William E. Tucker, *Journey in Faith: A History of the Christian Church (Disciples of Christ)* (St. Louis: Bethany Press, 1975), 290–91.

18. Schwantes, *Coxey's Army*, 188–89.

19. *Washington Post*, May 7, 1894, 1.

20. Hogan is chronicled in Schwantes, *Coxey's Army*, 149–65, 219–21, and McMurry, *Coxey's Army*, 199–206.

21. Schwantes, *Coxey's Army*, 161–62.

22. Gerald G. Eggert, *Richard Olney: Evolution of a Statesman* (University Park: Pennsylvania State University Press, 1974), 121–22.

23. Schwantes, *Coxey's Army*, 202; *New York Times*, April 29, 1894, 2; April 30, 1894, 5; *Washington Post*, April 29, 1894, 1.

24. Vincent, *Story of the Commonweal*, 195.

25. Schwantes, *Coxey's Army*, 186–87; McMurry, *Coxey's Army*, 229–32; Vincent, *Story of the Commonweal*, 174–98.

26. William O. Reichert, "The Melancholy Thought of Morrison I. Swift," *New England Quarterly* 49, no. 4 (1976): 543; *Washington Post*, February 21, 1894, 1; McMurry, *Coxey's Army*, 227–28.

27. *New York Times*, April 23, 1894, 1; April 29, 1894, 2.

28. Ibid., May 1, 1894, 2.

29. Schwantes, *Coxey's Army*, 264.

30. *Washington Post*, March 29, 1894, 2.

31. *New York Times*, April 2, 1894, 1.

32. A. Cleveland Hall, "An Observer in Coxey's Camp," *The Independent*, May 17, 1894, 3.

33. Matthew F. Griffin, "Secret Service Memories," part 1 of the Coxey portion, *Flynn's Weekly Detective Fiction* , March 13, 1926, 920.

34. H. L. Stetson, "The Industrial Army," *The Independent*, May 31, 1894, 5. McMurry attributes the figures to Aylesworth's students: *Coxey's Army*, 187–88.

35. William T. Stead, " 'Coxeyism': A Character Sketch," *Review of Reviews* 10, no. 1 (1894): 51–52. Hourwich's report is not extant; the figures are reported in the Stead article. Stead misspells Hourwich's name, but he is obviously referring to the noted Chicago-based scholar of the time.

36. "The Progress of the World," in *Review of Reviews* 10, no. 1 (1894): 4–5.

37. Baker, "Met by Armed Forces," *Chicago Record*, dateline April 24, 1894, *Coxey's Army, 1893–1894: Scrapbook with Photographs* (New York Public Library Photography Collection), 1:61.

38. Shirley Plumer Austin, "Coxey's Commonweal Army," *Chautauquan* 9, no. 3 (1894): 335.

39. Schwantes, *Coxey's Army*, 193.

40. "Diary of the March," *Chicago Record*, dateline April 20, 1894, *Coxey's Army: Scrapbook*, 1:77.

41. Michael C. Pierce, *Striking with the Ballot: Ohio Labor and the Populist Party* (DeKalb: Northern Illinois University Press, 2010), 163–64.

CHAPTER FIVE: Reception in the Capital

1. *Visitor's Companion at Our Nation's Capital* (Philadelphia: G. G. Evans, 1892); Alan Lessoff, *The Nation and Its City: Politics, Corruption, and Progress in Washington, DC, 1861–1902* (Baltimore: Johns Hopkins University Press, 1994).

2. Carlos Schwantes, *Coxey's Army: An American Odyssey* (Lincoln: University of Nebraska Press, 1985), 179–82; Donald L. McMurry, *Coxey's Army: A Study of the Industrial Army Movement of 1894* (1929; repr., New York: AMS Press, 1970), 116–22; Lucy Barber, *Marching on Washington: The Forging of an American Political Tradition* (Berkeley: University of California Press, 2002), 34–36; *Washington Post*, May 2, 1894, 1; Ray Stannard Baker, *American Chronicle* (New York: Charles Scribner's Sons, 1945), 24–25.

3. Baker, *American Chronicle*, 25.

4. *Washington Post*, May 3, 1894, 2.

5. *Congressional Record*, May 2, 1894, 4336; May 9, 1894, 4512.

6. Ibid., 4516.

7. Schwantes, *Coxey's Army*, 180; *Washington Post*, May 5, 1894, 8.

8. *Washington Post*, May 3, 1894, 1; May 5, 1894, 1; May 6, 1894, 2; Schwantes, *Coxey's Army*, 182.

9. *Washington Post*, May 8, 1894, 2; May 9, 1894, 1.

10. *New York Times*, May 10, 1894, 5.

11. *Washington Post*, May 10, 1894, 2.

12. Ibid., May 13, 1894, 2.

13. Ibid., May 14, 1894, 1.

14. Ibid., May 15, 1894, 2.

15. Ibid., May 16, 1894, 2; May 21, 1894, 1.

16. Ibid., May 22, 1894, 2.

17. Ibid., May 31, 1894, 4; June 11, 1894, 1; *Kalamazoo Gazette*, June 20, 1894, 7.

18. *Washington Post*, July 5, 1894, 2; Schwantes, *Coxey's Army*, 222; McMurry, *Coxey's Army*, 247.

19. Address of Eugene V. Debs at the Convention of the American Railway Union, June 12, 1894 (Terre Haute, IN: Moore & Langan, 1894), also printed in *Omaha World-Herald*, June 18, 1894, 5.

20. Stanley Buder, *Pullman: An Experiment in Industrial Order and Community Planning, 1880–1930* (New York: Oxford University Press, 1967); Gerald G. Eggert, *Richard Olney: Evolution of a Statesman* (University Park: Pennsylvania State University Press, 1974), 133–50; Baker, *American Chronicle*, 34–44.

21. John L. Thomas, *Alternative America: Henry George, Edward Bellamy, Henry Demarest Lloyd, and the Adversary Tradition* (Cambridge, MA: Belknap Press of Harvard University Press, 1983), 319.

22. *Washington Post*, May 30, 1894, 1; June 1, 1894, 2; June 12, 1894, 1; June 26, 1894. 2; Schwantes, *Coxey's Army*, 223–24.

23. *Washington Post*, June 18, 1894, 1; June 19, 1894, 1; August 14, 1894, 2.

24. Donald B. Smith, *Honoré Jaxon: Prairie Visionary* (Regina, SK: Coteau Books, 2007), 98–99.

25. *Grand Rapids Evening Press*, June 18, 1894, 1.

26. Schwantes, *Coxey's Army*, 246; *New York Times*, July 8, 1894, 7; *Washington Post*, July 26, 1894, 5.

27. Schwantes, *Coxey's Army*, 248–50; *Washington Post*, July 17, 1894, 2; July 19, 1894, 2.

28. *Washington Post*, July 18, 1894, 4.

29. Schwantes, *Coxey's Army*, 204–6.

30. Elizabeth Jameson, *All That Glitters: Class, Conflict, and Community in Cripple Creek* (Urbana: University of Illinois Press, 1998), 54–61.

31. Schwantes, *Coxey's Army*, 203–204; McMurry, *Coxey's Army*, 206–13.

32. *Washington Post*, August 10, 1894, 2.

33. Schwantes, *Coxey's Army*, 253; *Washington Post*, August 12, 1894, 2.

34. Schwantes, *Coxey's Army*, 254–55.

35. *Washington Post*, August 13, 1894, 2; August 14, 1894, 2; August 15, 1894, 5.

36. Ibid., August 15, 1894, 5.

37. Ibid., August 17, 1894, 5.

38. Ibid., August 18, 1894, 5; August 25, 1894, 8; *New York Times*, October 21, 1894, 8; Schwantes, *Coxey's Army*, 257–58.

EPILOGUE: Legacies and Enduring Questions

1. *Anglo-American Financial Agreement: Hearings Before the Committee on Banking and Currency, House of Representatives, Seventy-ninth Congress, Second Session, on H.J. Res. 311* (Washington, DC: U.S. Government Printing Office, 1946), 499–533; Embrey Bernard Howson, "Jacob Sechler Coxey: A Biography of a Monetary Reformer, 1854–1951" (PhD diss., Ohio State University, 1973, ohiolink.edu), passim.

2. Jacob Sechler Coxey Sr. Papers, box 4, folder 23, roll 4 on microfilm, Ohio Historical Society; *New York Times*, May 22, 1914, 16; *Washington Post*, March 13, 1914, 2, 10, 13; March 18, 1914, 3; Howson, "Jacob Sechler Coxey," 406–8.

3. *New York Times*, September 25, 1898, 2; *Washington Post*, May 19, 1951, 1; Jeff Miller, e-mail to the author, March 19, 2014; searches on Ancestry Library database.

4. *New York Times*, June 16, 1895. 24; July 16, 1896, 1; *Washington Post*, August 31, 1913, 2; January 17, 1914, 16; Jan. 24, 1914, 10; Carlos Schwantes, *Coxey's Army: An American Odyssey* (Lincoln: University of Nebraska Press, 1985), 258–59.

5. *Washington Post*, February 15, 1901, 4; May 19, 1951, 1; *New York Times*, May 21, 1951, 29; June 16, 1895, 24; Donald L. McMurry, *Coxey's Army: A Study of the Industrial Army Movement of 1894* (1929: repr., New York: AMS Press, 1970), 291; Jeff Davis, *The Devil on Wheels* (Cincinnati, OH: By the author, 1962), 74–76; Howson, "Jacob Sechler Coxey," passim.

6. Schwantes, *Coxey's Army*, 259; biographical information on Samuel Amos Pfrimmer, courtesy of e-mail to author from historian Samuel Pfrimmer Hays, May 5, 2012; Donald Smith, *Honoré Jaxon: Prairie Visionary* (Regina, SK: Coteau Books, 2007), 196–98.

7. Michael C. Pierce, *Striking with the Ballot: Ohio Labor and the Populist Party* (DeKalb: Northern Illinois University Press, 2010), 235.

8. Richard Schneirov, *Labor and Urban Politics: Class Conflict and the Origins of*

Modern Liberalism in Chicago, 1864–1897 (Urbana: University of Illinois Press, 1998), 343–56.

9. Pierce, *Striking with the Ballot*, 183–212; Charles Postel, *The Populist Vision* (New York: Oxford University Press, 2007), 269–75.

10. Pierce, *Striking with the Ballot*, 227–34.

11. Gerald G. Eggert, *Richard Olney: Evolution of a Statesman* (University Park: Pennsylvania State University Press, 1974), 151–69; Julie Greene, *Pure and Simple Politics: The American Federation of Labor and Political Activism, 1881–1917* (New York: Cambridge University Press, 1998), 97–104.

12. Chris Arnold, "Frustration Over Jobs Unites 'Occupiers' in Boston," *Morning Edition*, National Public Radio, October 21, 2011, http://www.npr.org.

13. Roy Jenkins, *Franklin Delano Roosevelt* (New York: Times Books, 2003), 63.

14. 409 U.S. 972 (1972).

15. Ronald J. Krotoszynski Jr., *Reclaiming the Petition Clause: Seditious Libel, "Offensive" Protest, and the Right to Petition the Government for a Redress of Grievances* (New Haven, CT: Yale University Press, 2002).

SUGGESTED FURTHER READING

Two full-length books by academic historians dedicated to the march of the Commonweal are Carlos Schwantes, *Coxey's Army: An American Odyssey* (Lincoln: University of Nebraska Press, 1985), and Donald L. McMurry, *Coxey's Army: A Study of the Industrial Army Movement of 1894* (1929; repr., New York: AMS Press, 1970). An important book-length narrative written and released while the story was in progress, by the official historian of the movement who was a noted Populist editor of the time, is Henry Vincent, *The Story of the Commonweal* (1894; repr., New York: Arno Press, 1969). Two important dissertations on Coxey are Embrey Bernard Howson, "Jacob Sechler Coxey: A Biography of a Monetary Reformer, 1854–1951" (Ohio State University, 1973, online at ohiolink.edu), and Jerry Prout, "Coxey's Challenge in the Populist Movement" (George Mason University, 2012); for a master's thesis on Coxey, see Edwin V. Pugh, "General J. S. Coxey, Politician" (University of Pittsburgh, 1948, online at massillonmuseum.org). For a half-hour documentary video, see *Coxey's Army* (Massillon Museum, 1894, online at massillonmuseum.org). Coxey and his associates also occupy a full chapter in Lucy Barber, *Marching on Washington: The Forging of an American Political Tradition* (Berkeley: University of California Press, 2002), which also contains valuable analysis of the subsequent protests in the capital; Errol Wayne Stevens, *Radical L.A.: From Coxey's Army to the Watts Riots, 1894–1965* (Norman: University of Oklahoma Press, 2009); and Russel B. Nye, *A Baker's Dozen: Thirteen Unusual Americans* (East Lansing: Michigan State University Press, 1956). Journal articles dealing with specific components or aspects of the Coxey march include Michael Barkun, "Coxey's Army as a Millennial Movement," *Religion* 18, no. 4 (1988): 363–89; Thomas A. Clinch, "Coxey's Army in Montana," *Montana: The Magazine of Western History* 15, no. 4 (1965): 2–11; and Henry Winfred Splitter, "Concerning Vinette's Los Angeles Regiment of Coxey's Army," *Pacific Historical Review* 17, no. 1 (1948): 29–36. Michael S. Sweeney studies the role of the press with the Coxey episode in "'The Desire for the Sensational': Coxey's Army and the Argus-Eyed Demons of Hell," *Journalism History* 23, no. 3 (1997): 114–25. The army's role in the affair is discussed in Jerry M. Cooper, *The Army and Civil Disorder: Federal Military Intervention in Labor Disputes, 1877–1900* (Westport, CT: Greenwood Press, 1890).

For information on Honoré Jaxon, see Donald Smith, *Honoré Jaxon: Prairie Visionary* (Regina, SK: Coteau Books, 2007); on Morrison I. Swift, see William O. Reichert, "The Melancholy Thought of Morrison I. Swift," *New England Quarterly* 49, no.4 (1976): 524–58. Mary P. Ryan gives context to the role of pristinely dressed women in nineteenth-century parades with *Women in Public: Between Banners and Ballots, 1825–1880* (Baltimore: Johns Hopkins University Press, 1990). For insight into the spiritual beliefs that Carl Browne adapted for himself and Coxey, see Bruce F. Campbell, *Ancient Wisdom Revived: A History of the Theosophical Movement* (Berkeley: University of California Press, 1980), and, for the viewpoint of the founder herself, Helena Petrovna Blavatsky, *The Key to Theosophy* (London: Theosophical Publishing, 1893). On Coxey's town, see Margy Vogt, *Towpath to Towpath: Massillon, Ohio* (Massillon, OH: Bates Printing, 2002). Popular magazine articles on the Coxey march include George A. Gipe, "Rebel in a White Collar," *American Heritage* 18, no. 1 (1966): 25–29, and Joseph Gustaitis, "Coxey's Army," *American History Illustrated* 29, no. 1 (1994): 38–45.

The Jacob Sechler Coxey Sr. Papers, which contain a small amount of material about the 1894 march (mostly newspaper clippings and one letter Coxey wrote from jail) and more about Coxey's later endeavors and family relationships, are housed at the Massillon Museum in Massillon, OH. Microfilm of the papers, made in 1971 and therefore not including materials added since them, is available at the Ohio Historical Society. Research for this book also included a look at the papers of Richard Olney, Grover Cleveland, and Ray Stannard Baker, all at the Library of Congress, Washington, DC.

The richest of primary sources about the day-to-day adventures of the Commonweal are newspaper articles, a huge trove of which can be brought up by running Coxey's name through a library database, e.g., America's Historical Newspapers, or the database of a specific major paper. The *Washington Post* was most helpful to this work. While the relevant articles are far too numerous to list (lengthy updates appeared daily for much of the year), one should note a few that contain special information: "Remnant of Coxey's Army," October 18, 1903, E-11; "Keeping Tab on Coxey," January 11, 1897, 10; "Last of a Noted 'Wealer,'" August 18, 1895, 1; "Capital Detectives Tell How, Disguised as Hoboes, They Watched Coxey's Army," September 3, 1922, 22. Matthew F. Griffin recalls his time with the army as a Secret Service spy in "Secret Service Memories" (two parts of a larger serial), *Flynn's Weekly Detective Fiction* 13 (March 13, 1926): 906–27 and 14 (March 20, 1926): 86–98. Jack London's experience marching with the Kelleyites can be found in *Jack London on the Road: The Tramp Diary and Other Hobo Writings*, ed. Richard W. Etulain (Logan: Utah State University Press, 1979).

Works containing commentaries on the march written by its contemporaries include James P. Boyd, *Vital Questions of the Day* (New York: Publishers Union, 1894); Ray Stannard Baker, *American Chronicle* (New York: Charles Scribner's Sons, 1945); Shirley Austen Plumer, "Coxey's Commonweal Army," *Chautauquan* 19, no. 3 (1894): 332–36, and Plumer, "The Downfall of Coxeyism," *Chautauquan* 19, no. 4 (1894): 448–52; A. Cleveland Hall, "An Observer in Coxey's Camp," *The Independent*, May 17, 1894, 3–4; "The Progress of the World," *Review of Reviews* 10, no. 1 (1894): 4–5, William T. Stead, "'Coxeyism': A Character Sketch," in ibid., 47–59, and "The Coxey

Crusade," in ibid., 63–66 (Stead is decisively more sympathetic to Coxey than the journal's editors); Oliver Otis Howard, Thomas Byrnes, and Alvah H. Doty, "The Menace of 'Coxeyism,'" *North American Review* 158, no. 451 (1894): 687–705; Thorstein Veblen, "The Army of the Commonweal," *Journal of Political Economy* 2, no. 3 (1894): 456–61; and H. L. Stetson, "The Industrial Army," *The Independent*, May 31, 1894, 5. Many of the period's magazines are available at major libraries through the databases American Periodicals and HathiTrust. For Coxey's own outlook on both the 1894 and the 1914 marches, see *Coxey: His Own Story of the Commonweal* (printed by author, 1914, online at massillonmuseum.org). Ray Stannard Baker's articles in the *Chicago Record* from the 1894 march, as well as many photographs and other Coxey-related resources, are preserved in the two-volume *Coxey's Army, 1893–1894: Scrapbook with Photographs* in the New York Public Library's Photography Collection.

Local studies and portraits of regions where Coxey-related events occurred, and communities the Coxeyites encountered, include Elizabeth Jameson, *All That Glitters: Class, Conflict, and Community in Cripple Creek* (Urbana: University of Illinois Press, 1998); Thomas G. Alexander, "Ogden, a Federal Colony in Utah," *Utah Historical Quarterly* 47, no. 3 (1979): 291–309; Edward Steven Slavishak, *Bodies of Work: Civil Display and Labor in Industrial Pittsburgh* (Durham, NC: Duke University Press, 2008); Robert J. Brugger, *Maryland: A Middle Temperament, 1634–1980* (Baltimore: Johns Hopkins University Press, 1988); Edward Leo Lyman, *Political Deliverance: The Mormon Quest for Utah Statehood* (Urbana: University of Illinois Press, 1986); Richard Warner and Ryan Roenfeld, *Council Bluffs Broadway* (Charleston, SC: Arcadia Publishing, 2007); David L. Bristow, *A Dirty Wicked Town: Tales of 19th-Century Omaha* (Caldwell, ID: Caxton Press, 2000); John Archibald Bole, *The Harmony Society: A Chapter in German American Culture History*, PhD diss. (University of Pennsylvania, 1904, accessible at books.google.com); and Lester G. McAllister and William E. Tucker, *Journey in Faith: A History of the Christian Church (Disciples of Christ)* (St. Louis: Bethany Press, 1975).

For a spotlight on Chicago, see Richard Schneirov, *Labor and Urban Politics: Class Conflict and the Origins of Modern Liberalism in Chicago, 1864–1897* (Urbana: University of Illinois Press, 1998); Huping Ling, *Chinese Chicago: Race, Transcontinental Migration, and Community since 1870* (Stanford, CA: Stanford University Press, 2012); and Ray Ginger, *Altgeld's America, 1890–1905* (1958; Chicago: Quadrangle, 1965). For information on late-nineteenth-century Washington, DC, see De B. Randolph Keim, *Keim's Illustrated Hand-book: Washington and Its Environs, a Descriptive and Historical Hand-book of the Capital of the United States of America* (Washington, DC: printed by author, 1886); *Visitor's Companion at Our Nation's Capital* (Philadelphia: G. G. Evans, 1892); Alan Lessoff, *The Nation and Its City: Politics, Corruption, and Progress in Washington, DC, 1861–1902* (Baltimore: Johns Hopkins University Press, 1994); Carl Abbott: *Political Terrain: Washington, DC, from Tidewater Town to Global Metropolis* (Chapel Hill: University of North Carolina Press 1999); Constance McLaughlin Green, *Secret City: A History of Race Relations in the Nation's Capital* (Princeton, NJ: Princeton University Press, 1967); Kate Masur, *An Example for All the Land: Emancipation and the*

Struggle over Equality in Washington, D.C. (Chapel Hill: University of North Carolina Press, 2010); and Allan John Johnston, *Surviving Freedom: The Black Community of Washington, D.C., 1860–1880* (New York: Garland, 1993).

Important overall works covering life, technology, politics, and ideas in the Gilded Age include John A. Garraty, *The New Commonwealth, 1877–1890* (New York: Harper & Row, 1968); Harold Underwood Faulkner, *Politics, Reform, and Expansion, 1890–1900* (New York: Harper, 1959); Samuel P. Hays, *The Response to Industrialism, 1885–1914*, 2nd ed. (Chicago: University of Chicago Press, 1995); Nell Irvin Painter, *Standing at Armageddon: The United States, 1877–1919* (New York: W. W. Norton, 1987); Alan Trachtenberg, *The Incorporation of America: Culture and Society in the Gilded Age* (New York: Hill & Wang, 1982); Rebecca Edwards, *New Spirits: Americans in the Gilded Age, 1865–1905* (New York: Oxford University Press, 2006); Robert H. Walker, *Everyday Life in the Age of Enterprise, 1865–1900* (New York: Putman, 1967); Robert H. Wiebe, *The Search for Order, 1877–1920* (New York: Hill & Wang, 1967); H. W. Brands, *The Reckless Decade: America in the 1890s* (New York: St. Martin's Press, 1995); and Raymond A. Mohl, *The New City: Urban America in the Industrial Age, 1860–1920* (Wheeling, IL: Harlan Davidson, 1985).

Volumes dedicated to Gilded Age politics include Robert W. Cherny, *American Politics in the Gilded Age* (Wheeling, IL: Harlan Davidson, 1997); Charles W. Calhoun, *From Bloody Shirt to Full Dinner Pail: The Transformation of Politics and Governance in the Gilded Age* (New York: Hill & Wang, 2010); John M. Dobson, *Politics in the Gilded Age: A New Perspective on Reform* (New York: Praeger, 1972); and Michael E. McGerr, *The Decline of Popular Politics: The North, 1865–1928* (New York: Oxford University Press, 1986). Among the books that explore the precursors to Coxey's monetary theories are Irwin Unger, *The Greenback Era: A Social and Political History of American Finance, 1865–1879* (Princeton, NJ: Princeton University Press, 1968); Robert H. Walker, *Reform in America: The Continuing Frontier* (Lexington: University Press of Kentucky, 1985); Gretchen Ritter, *Goldbugs and Greenbacks: The Antimonopoly Tradition and the Politics of Finance in America* (New York: Cambridge University Press, 1997); and Charles M. Destler, *American Radicalism, 1865–1901: Essays and Documents* (New York: Octagon Books, 1963). Much vital information as well as key documents can be found in the multi-volume *History of American Presidential Elections, 1789–2001*, ed. Arthur M. Schlesinger Jr. (Philadelphia: Chelsea House, 2002).

Editions of primary sources from the time cited in this work include Henry George, *Progress and Poverty: An Inquiry into the Cause of Industrial Depressions and of Increase of Want with Increase of Wealth; The Remedy* (1879; repr., New York: Robert Schalkenbach Foundation, 1971); Edward Bellamy, *Looking Backward, 2000–1887* (1887; repr., New York: Signet, 2009); William Graham Sumner, *What Social Classes Owe to Each Other* (1883; repr., Caldwell, ID: Caxton, 1966); and Mark Twain and Charles Dudley Warner, *The Gilded Age: A Tale of To-day* (1873, repr., Indianapolis: Bobbs-Merrill, 1872).

Works more specifically about technology, production, and corporate structures in the Gilded Age include Richard White, *Railroaded: The Transcontinentals and the*

Making of Modern America (New York: W. W. Norton, 2011); Glenn Porter, *The Rise of Big Business*, 3rd ed. (Wheeling, IL: Harlan Davidson, 2005); David A. Hounshell, *From the American System to Mass Production, 1800–1932: The Development of Manufacturing Technology in the United States* (Baltimore: Johns Hopkins University Press, 1985); Alfred D. Chandler, *The Visible Hand: The Managerial Revolution in American Business* (Cambridge, MA: Harvard University Press, 1977); Richard B. Du Boff, "The Telegraph in Nineteenth-Century America," *Comparative Studies in Society and History* 26, no. 4 (1984): 571–86. Walter Licht, *Industrializing America: The Nineteenth Century* (Baltimore: Johns Hopkins University Press, 1995); Thomas Kessner, *Capital City: New York City and the Men Behind America's Rise to Economic Dominance, 1860–1900* (New York: Oxford University Press, 2005); Charles R. Morris, *The Tycoons: How Andrew Carnegie, John D. Rockefeller, Jay Gould, and J. P. Morgan Invented the American Supereconomy* (New York: Times Books, 2005); and H. W. Brands, *American Colossus: The Triumph of Capitalism, 1865–1900* (New York: Doubleday, 2010).

On western expansion and the plight of Native Americans, see Richard White, *"It's Your Misfortune and None of My Own": A History of the American West* (Norman: University of Oklahoma Press, 1991); Frederick E. Hoxie, *A Final Promise: The Campaign to Assimilate the Indians, 1880–1920* (Lincoln: University of Nebraska Press, 1984); Patricia Nelson Limerick, *The Legacy of Conquest: The Unbroken Past of the American West* (New York: W. W. Norton, 1987), and *Something in the Soil: Legacies and Reckonings in the New West* (New York: W. W. Norton, 2000); and Roy Morris Jr., *Sheridan: The Life and Wars of General Phil Sheridan* (New York: Crown Publishers, 1992).

The late nineteenth century can scarcely be understood without reference to the American Civil War and its aftermath, especially with regard to race, racial politics, and the lives of African Americans. A list of important works on those themes would run longer than this book, but a sampling includes James McPherson, *Battle Cry of Freedom* (New York: Oxford University Press, 1988); Bruce Levine, *The Fall of the House of Dixie: The Civil War and the Social Revolution That Transformed the South* (New York: Random House, 2013); Eric Foner, *Reconstruction: America's Unfinished Revolution* (New York: Harper & Row, 1988); Grace Elizabeth Hale, *Making Whiteness: The Culture of Segregation in the South, 1890–1940* (New York: Pantheon Books, 1998); and David W. Blight, *Race and Reunion: The Civil War in American Memory* (Cambridge, MA: Harvard University Press, 2001).

Studies of ideas about the social implications of industrial capitalism include Robert H. Walker, *The Poet and the Gilded Age: Social Themes in Late 19th- Century American Verse* (New York: Octagon Books, 1969); John L. Thomas, *Alternative America: Henry George, Edward Bellamy, Henry Demarest Lloyd, and the Adversary Tradition* (Cambridge, MA: Belknap Press of Harvard University Press, 1983); John F. Kasson, *Civilizing the Machine: Technology and Republican Values in America* (New York: Grossman, 1976); Gerald N. Grob, *Workers and Utopia: A Study of Ideological Conflict in the American Labor Movement* (Evanston, IL: Northwestern University Press,1961); Bruce Curtis, *William Graham Sumner* (Boston: Twayne, 1981). For social welfare policies and local relief efforts in the nineteenth century, see Michael B. Katz, *In* the Shadow of the Poorhouse: A Social History of Welfare in America (New York: Basic Books, 1986); Todd DePastino, Citizen Hobo: How a Century of Homelessness Shaped America (Chicago: University of Chicago Press, 2003); Sidney Fine, Laissez-Faire and the General-Welfare State: A Study of Conflict in American Thought (Ann Arbor: University of Michigan Press, 1956); and Leah Hannah Feder, Unemployment Relief in Periods of Depression: A Study of Measures Adopted in Certain American Cities, 1857 through 1922 (New York: Russell Sage Foundation, 1936). For the labor protests demanding public works projects in 1873–74, see two articles by Herbert G. Gutman: "The Failure of the Movement by the Unemployment for Public Works in 1873," Political Science Quarterly 80, no. 2 (1965): 254–76, and "The Tompkins Square 'Riot' in New York City on January 13, 1874: A Re-Examination of Its Causes and Its Aftermath," Labor History 6, no. 1 (1965): 44–70.

A tiny sampling of the significant works of labor history for the Gilded Age includes Melvyn Dubofsky, Industrialism and the American Worker, 1865–1920, 3rd ed. (Wheeling, IL: Harlan Davidson, 1996); Bruce Laurie, Artisans into Workers: Labor in Nineteenth-Century America (New York: Hill & Wang, 1989); Philip S. Foner, History of the Labor Movement in the United States, especially volumes 1 and 2 (New York: International Publishers, 1947) ; Stanley Buder, Pullman: An Experiment in Industrial Order and Community Planning, 1880–1930 (New York: Oxford University Press, 1967); and Julie Greene, Pure and Simple Politics: The American Federation of Labor and Political Activism, 1881–1917 (New York: Cambridge University Press, 1998). Specifically on the Knights of Labor, see Kim Voss, The Making of American Exceptionalism: The Knights of Labor and Class Formation in the Nineteenth Century (Ithaca, NY: Cornell University Press, 1993); Leon Fink, Workingmen's Democracy: The Knights of Labor and American Politics (Urbana: University of Illinois Press, 1985); and Robert E. Weir, Knights Unhorsed: Internal Conflict in a Gilded Age Social Movement (Detroit: Wayne State University Press, 2000). Books on specific episodes of labor conflict include Paul Krause, The Battle for Homestead, 1880–1892 (Pittsburgh: University of Pittsburgh Press, 1992); James R. Green, Death in the Haymarket: A Story of Chicago, the First Labor Movement, and the Bombing That Divided Gilded Age America (New York: Pantheon Books, 2006); and Paul Avrich, The Haymarket Tragedy (Princeton, NJ: Princeton University Press, 1984). Timothy Messer-Kruse offers a provocative reassessment of longstanding beliefs about Haymarket in The Trial of the Haymarket Anarchists: Terrorism and Justice in the Gilded Age (New York: Palgrave Macmillian, 2011).

Among the many important biographies and autobiographies of labor leaders are Samuel Gompers, Seventy Years of Life and Labor, 2 vols. (New York: E. P. Dutton, 1925); Bernard Mandel, Samuel Gompers: A Biography (Yellow Springs, OH: Antioch, 1963); Stuart Bruce Kaufman, Samuel Gompers and the Origins of the American Federation of Labor, 1848–1896 (Westport, CT: Greenwood, 1973); Craig Phelan, Grand Master Workman: Terence Powderly and the Knights of Labor (Westport, CT: Greenwood, 2000); Ray Ginger, The Bending Cross: A Biography of Eugene V. Debs (New Brunswick, NJ: Rutgers University Press, 1949); and Nick Salvatore, Eugene V. Debs: Citizen and Socialist (Urbana: University of Illinois Press, 1982). On Gompers, see also The Samuel

Gompers Papers, especially volume 3, ed. Stuart B. Kaufman (Urbana: University of Illinois Press, 1989). Edward O'Donnell delves into the work of Henry George with his brand-new book *The True Republic of the Future: Henry George, the Great Upheaval, and the Republican Crisis of the Gilded Age* (New York: Columbia University Press, forthcoming in 2015). The present work cites quotations from his dissertation, "Henry George and the 'New Political Forces': Ethnic Nationalism, Labor Radicalism, and Politics in Gilded Age New York City," PhD diss., Columbia University, 1995. An important work on the life of another reformer of the era is Charles M. Destler, *Henry Demarest Lloyd and the Empire of Reform* (Philadelphia: University of Pennsylvania Press, 1963), and one on a contemporary radical is L. Glen Seretan, *Daniel DeLeon: Odyssey of an American Marxist* (Cambridge, MA: Harvard University Press, 1979).

Among the many important scholarly studies of the rise of Populism are Lawrence Goodwyn, *Democratic Promise: The Populist Moment in America* (New York: Oxford University Press, 1976); Robert C. McMath Jr., *American Populism: A Social History, 1877–1898* (New York: Hill & Wang, 1993); Charles Postel, *The Populist Vision* (New York: Oxford University Press, 2007); James M. Beeby, ed., *Populism in the South Revisited: New Interpretations and New Departures* (Jackson: University Press of Mississippi, 2012); John Donald Hicks, *The Populist Revolt: A History of the Farmers' Alliance and the People's Party* (Lincoln: University of Nebraska Press, 1961); Norman Pollack, *The Populist Response to Industrial America: Midwestern Political Thought* (New York: W. W. Norton, 1966); Carleton Beals, *The Great Revolt and Its Leaders: The History of Popular American Uprisings in the 1890s* (London: Abelard-Schuman, 1968); Gene Clanton, *Congressional Populism and the Crisis of the 1890s* (Lawrence: University Press of Kansas, 1998); and Peter H. Argersinger, *Populism and Politics: William Alfred Peffer and the People's Party* (Lexington: University Press of Kentucky, 1974). For African American political experiences and the racial dimensions to the labor struggles, see Omar H. Ali, *In the Lion's Mouth: Black Populism in the New South, 1886–1900* (Jackson: University Press of Mississippi, 2010); Steven Hahn, *A Nation under Our Feet: Black Political Struggles in the Rural South from Slavery to the Great Migration* (Cambridge, MA: Harvard University Press, 2003); Joseph Gerteis, *Class and the Color Line: Interracial Class Coalition in the Knights of Labor and the Populist Movement* (Durham, NC: Duke University Press, 2007); and William H. Harris, *The Harder We Run: Black Workers since the Civil War* (New York: Oxford University Press, 1982). For populism in a long-term context, see Michael Kazin, *The Populist Persuasion: An American History* (New York: Basic Books, 1995). Connections between populism and broader reformism are explored in Michael C. Pierce, *Striking with the Ballot: Ohio Labor and the Populist Party* (DeKalb: Northern Illinois University Press, 2010); Matthew Hild, *Greenbackers, Knights of Labor, and Populists: Farmer-Labor Insurgency in the Late-Nineteenth-Century South* (Athens: University of Georgia Press, 2007); and *The Pullman Strike and the Crisis of the 1890s: Essays on Labor and Politics*, ed. Richard Schneirov, Shelton Stromquist, and Nick Salvatore (Urbana: University of Illinois Press, 1999).

Important works on the careers of leading politicians of national or local significance in the 1890s include Richard E. Welch, *The Presidencies of Grover Cleveland*

(Lawrence: University Press of Kansas, 1988); Gerald G. Eggert, *Richard Olney: Evolution of a Statesman* (University Park: Pennsylvania State University Press, 1974); H. Wayne Morgan, *William McKinley and His America*, 2nd ed. (Kent, OH: Kent State University Press, 2003); Willis J. Abbot, *Carter Henry Harrison: A Memoir* (New York: Dodd Mead, 1894); Claudius Osborne Johnson, *Carter Henry Harrison I: Political Leader* (Chicago: University of Chicago Press, 1928); and Robert Crawford Cotner, *James Stephen Hogg: A Biography* (Austin: University of Texas Press, 1959).

On the World's Fair of 1894, see Robert W. Rydell, *All the World's a Fair: Visions of Empire at American International Expositions, 1876–1916* (Chicago: University of Chicago Press, 1984), and Erik Larson, *The Devil in the White City: A Saga of Magic and Murder at the Fair That Changed America* (New York: Vintage, 2004). Book-length studies specifically about the economic crisis of the 1890s include Douglas W. Steeples and David O. Whitten, *Democracy in Desperation: The Depression of 1893* (Westport, CT: Greenwood Press, 1998), and Samuel T. McSeveney, *The Politics of Depression: Political Behavior in the Northeast, 1893–1896* (New York: Oxford University Press, 1972). Two key journal articles with same focus are Samuel Rezneck, "Unemployment, Unrest, and Relief in the United States, during the Depression of 1893–1897," *Journal of Political Economy* 61, no. 4 (1953): 324–45, and Charles Hoffman, "The Depression of the Nineties," *Journal of Economic History* 16, no. 2 (1956): 137–64. Closely related is Sidney L. Harring, "Class Conflict and the Suppression of Tramps in Buffalo, 1892–1894," *Law and Society Review* 11, no. 5 (1977): 873–911. Contemporary primary sources with further details on poverty and relief in the crisis of the 1890s include Carlos C. Closson Jr., "The Unemployed in American Cities," *Quarterly Review of Economics* 8, no. 2 (1894): 168–217; Josephine Shaw Lowell, "Methods of Relief for the Unemployed," *Forum* 16 (February 1894): 655–62; J. J. McCook, "A Tramp Census and Its Revelation," *Forum* 15 (August 1893): 753–66; Edward W. Bemis, "The Convention of the American Federation of Labor," *Journal of Political Economy* 2, no. 2 (1894): 298–99; and William T. Stead, *If Christ Came to Chicago* (Chicago: Laird & Lee, 1894, accessed at books.google.com). A noteworthy work on depressions in general, including the 1890s crisis, is Charles P. Kindleberger, *Manias, Panics, and Crashes: A History of Financial Crises*, 4th ed. (New York: John Wiley & Sons, 2000).

Works showing how the issues of Coxey's time played themselves out in the century that followed include John Milton Cooper, *Pivotal Decades: 1900–1920* (New York: W. W. Norton, 1990); Michael E. Parrish, *Anxious Decades: America in Prosperity and Depression, 1920–1941* (New York: W. W. Norton, 1992); David M. Kennedy, *Freedom from Fear: The American People in Depression and War, 1929–1945* (New York: Oxford University Press, 1999); Anthony J. Badger, *The New Deal: The Depression Years, 1933–1940* (Basingstoke, UK: Palgrave Macmillan, 1989); William E. Leuchtenburg, *Franklin D. Roosevelt and the New Deal* (New York: Harper & Row, 1963); Charles Poor Kindleberger, *The World in Depression, 1929–1939* (Berkeley: University of California Press, 1973); Alonzo Hamby, *For the Survival of Democracy: Franklin Roosevelt and the World Crisis of the 1930s* (New York: Free Press, 2004); Alonzo Hamby, *Liberalism and Its Challengers: From F.D.R. to Bush*, 2nd ed. (New York: Oxford University

Press,1992); Joseph Finkelstein, *The American Economy: From the Great Crash to the Third Industrial Revolution* (Wheeling, IL: Harlan Davidson, 1992); James T. Patterson, *Grand Expectations: Postwar America, 1945–1974* (New York: Oxford University Press, 1995); and Ronald J. Krotoszynski Jr., *Reclaiming the Petition Clause: Seditious Libel, "Offensive" Protest, and the Right to Petition the Government for a Redress of Grievances* (New Haven, CT: Yale University Press, 2002).

INDEX

Swift, Augustus, 6
Swift, Morrison I., 92–93

Taft, President William Howard, 123
tariffs, 24, 31, 34, 112
taxation, 12, 29, 35, 36, 99, 125. *See also* George,
    Henry; income tax, graduated; Single Taxers
telegraph, 30, 65, 77, 91; ownership of, 26,
    42–43, 93; role in press coverage of Coxey's
    Army, 47, 48, 55–56. *See also* Western Union
Texas, 23, 25, 32, 77, 78–79, 80, 94
Texas seed bill, Cleveland veto of, 23–24, 25
Thayer, John J., 49, 63
"Tooting" Charley, 54, 67
"tramps," 10–11, 17, 35, 36, 37–38, 73, 79, 80,
    90, 93, 94, 95, 111, 114; "tramp laws," 11. *See
    also* unemployed
Treasury, U.S. Department of, 2, 34, 45, 74
Twain, Mark, 5–6

unemployed, 1, 3, 34–35, 37–38, 40, 49, 50,
    56, 57, 81, 87, 89–90, 92, 94, 109; attitudes
    toward, 10, 11–12, 13, 35–36, 37–38, 99, 101,
    112, 125; protests of, 1–3, 11–12, 13, 36, 40,
    42, 44, 58, 76–77, 80, 93, 96, 120, 125–26;
    relief for, 21, 34–35, 35–36, 43, 45–46, 69, 77,
    124. *See also* unemployment
unemployment, 2, 3, 12, 33, 35–37, 40, 43, 126.
    See also unemployed
Union Labor Party, 17, 27. *See also* George,
    Henry
United Mine Workers of America, 2, 38, 67.
    See also coal; gold; labor; McBride, John
University of Chicago, 94
Utah: statehood for, 8; Territory, 81–83

Vincent, Cuthbert, 27
Vincent, Henry, 27, 40, 48, 52, 92
Vincent, Leo, 27
Vinette, Arthur, 76, 80
Virginia, 68, 110, 111, 114–15

Wagner Act. *See* National Labor Relations Act
Waite, Gov. Davis, 31, 83, 91–92, 113
Walker, Robert, 33
Wall Street, 33, 34, 40, 110–11, 116
War, U.S. Department of, 29, 127
Warner, Charles Dudley, 5
Washington, DC, 119; Coxeyites in, 1–2, 50,
    74, 80, 90, 96, 97–103, 104, 106–7, 115, 116
    ; description of, 97; federal government in,
    24, 32, 34, 52, 58, 63, 69–70, 88, 112, 117–18,
    122–23; marches to, 36, 44–45, 46–47, 61,
    62, 67, 70–71, 76–77, 81, 82, 87, 92–95, 112,
    118, 126–27; police preparations, 56, 68–69,
    95. *See also* Maryland; police, in Washing-
    ton, DC; Virginia
Washington Post, 46, 49, 55, 65, 68, 72, 79, 94,
    104, 106, 110, 111, 114. *See also* press
Wayland, Francis, 11, 93
Wealth against Commonwealth (Lloyd), 42
Weaver, James B., 29, 31, 86–87, 121
welfare policies and proposals, 4, 10, 12, 23–24,
    32, 35–37, 58, 124–25, 126. *See also* unem-
    ployed, relief for
West, Gov. Caleb, 82
Western Union, 6
Weston, IA, 84
West Virginia, 49, 68, 80
Wheeling, WV, 80
Whitney, Eli, 7
Willard, Frances, 28
Wilson, President Woodrow, 123, 124
Women's Christian Temperance Union, 28. *See
    also* temperance
women: suffrage campaigns, 22, 27, 28, 124;
    supporting Coxeyites, 57, 66, 84, 98–99
World War I, 123, 126, 127
World War II, 118–19, 127
Wyoming, 82, 83, 84

Yale University, 20, 93; Law School, 11, 93